DIGITAL

LITERACY FOR

SENIOR CITIZENS

DIGITAL
LITERACY FOR
SENIOR
CITIZENS

Empowering Citizens

S.P. MANCHANDA

Published Internationally by

 **Pendown** Press

Powered by G Gullybaba

PENDOWN PRESS

Powered by **Gullybaba Publishing House Pvt. Ltd.,**
An ISO 9001 & ISO 14001 Certified Co.,
Regd. Office: 2525/193, 1st Floor, Onkar Nagar-A, Tri Nagar,
Delhi-110035
Ph.: 09350849407, 09312235086
E-mail: info@pendownpress.com
Branch Office: 1A/2A, 20, Hari Sadan, Ansari Road,
Daryaganj, New Delhi-110002
Ph.: 011-45794768
Website: PendownPress.com

First Edition: 2021
Price: ₹259/-
ISBN: 978-93-90828-43-2

DEDICATION

I dedicate this book to you, all my elderly friends. May you apply the life lessons you discover within these pages to manifest the fullness of your experience while making a difference in your life and the lives of the people at large.

This book is also dedicated to my late beloved wife, Smt. Usha Rani Manchanda, my entire family, especially my daughter Deepika and my son Ankit, the two of my greatest teachers.

POSITIVE FEEDBACK OF PREVIOUS BOOK

"Embrace your Own Power to Fight Corruption"

"It's heart-warming to see people of India in their post-retirement age talking about real issues and most importantly, effective solutions to solve those issues."

"This is a nicely-written book with all the important points jotted together. The real-time examples given in the book state how the common problems related to Govt.departments can be simply resolved by us without just cribbing about them..."

"This book is very encouraging. Easy to understand; I got to learn a lot through this book, every aspect is explained very well...."

"...And your good self has taken up the remedial measures for uplifting the society for the cause of smooth and happy living..."

"...Those who cry from the top of houses that RTI is causing blackmail and creating a new profession called RTI Activists who 'abuse' and 'extort', should read this book and talk to this active-author senior citizen. Then, they will certainly feel ashamed of what they are propagating. If one Manchanda emerges from each of every five to ten lakh people of India, the administrators shall wake up, politicians with bad motives will pack up and the worse systems will break up…"

CONTENTS

Foreword   i

About the Author and the Book   iii

Acknowledgements   viii

Purpose of writing this book   x

01	Digital literacy: An Introduction	1
02	Understanding Computers	4
03	Smartphones Guide for Elders	21
04	Social Networking	26
05	Online Communications	41
06	Useful Apps for Senior Citizens	53
07	Online & Mobile Banking	95
08	Digital Wellness & Cyber Security	109

FOREWORD

Helping Elders become Digitally Literate:
Leading the Way

It is truly commendable to see Mr. S.P. Manchanda leading the way to give our senior citizens a tool of independence and empowerment. This book on Digital Literacy for Senior Citizens is much needed in today's scenario. With the growing pace of technology and focus on Digital India, our elders are often left with the challenge of coping with the ever changing digital space.

The Covid-19 pandemic has affected senior citizens in several ways, such as health wise, economically, psychologically and even socially. Identified as one of the most vulnerable groups, they faced numerous challenges. Most could no longer carry on their daily living activities, whether it be going to the bank to manage their finances or going to the market to purchase fresh food or ration, or simply meet & connect with their loved ones. Lack of digital knowledge, has amplified the problem. Therefore, many seniors have shown interest to equip them with the knowledge and become digitally literate, so they can lead active and independent lives.

At HelpAge India, we conduct Digital Literacy workshops to help our elders become digitally literate, teaching them how to use smart phones, do online banking, helping them understand social networking, pay their utility bills, order daily essentials, participate in online classes and even do online shopping. It is important that in later years, one keeps themselves active both in mind and body. As they say, only a healthy mind can house a healthy body. Digital connectivity will go a long way in keeping our seniors both mentally and physically active.

It is therefore heartening to see Manchanda come out with a book to help our elders get digitally active and independent, helping them transform their lives, so they can stay engaged and empowered.

A senior citizen himself, he has truly taken the second innings of his life as a means to 'pay it forward' and help his peers. I wish him all the best in his future endeavors and hope that this book will go a long way in helping our senior citizens.

Rohit Prasad
Chief Executive Officer, HelpAge India
(Working for the cause and care of older persons)
December 2020

ABOUT THE AUTHOR
AND THE BOOK

Who says activism and the willingness to change society is only for the young and feisty? Senior citizens who have truly taken to a retired life may have some free time on their hands even if they are running errands and socializing. As we grow older, we see more of the world and have a much more stable view of the world than what we had in our early years. This is why seniors with a clear view of the world and enormous experience have a greater chance of making a difference.

Mr. Suraj Parkash Manchanda is a 68-year-old retired accomplished banker and a devoted social activist. Post his voluntary retirement in 2007; he dedicated his life to a social cause which includes empowering the senior citizens in India by motivating them to be digitally literate, teaching Consumer Protection Act & RTI Act to prevent corruption and most importantly, using creative writing as a tool to curb corruption. While Acts are enablers, he believes in thoughtful writing to ensure that he asks the right questions to generate the right insights from the responses. He has put his creativity to use in many positive and effective ways.

His art of using the RTI Act as a tool to plug loopholes and curb corruption in the system is being keenly observed and appreciated in judicial, legislative, and bureaucratic circles. He has written hundreds of RTI-petitions on many burning issues like corruption, black money in immovable properties, cardiac stent prices, MRP of essential drugs, medical negligence, etc. Central Information Commission (CIC) verdicts on his public-interest RTI petitions are automatically picked up by the media because of the importance attached to the issues involved in his petitions.

After getting desired information under RTI Act, he became busy filing Public Interest Litigation (PIL) in the High Court of Delhi in larger public interest issues. He has filed PIL against summer vacations in courts giving cogent arguments that long vacation means no entry for litigants for a long period. Given the pending cases in various courts, it no longer seems judicious to send officers and advocates of the court on long tours letting them enjoy their summers in air-conditioned rooms or at hill stations. He has also filed PIL in Delhi High Court against irrational government minimum rates (circle rates) of immovable properties which encourage corruption and black money transactions. The High Court has issued notice to the Govt. of NCT of Delhi and subsequently counsel for the respondent Govt. admitted anomalies. Hopefully, we will soon get revised circle rates calculated on a scientific basis, thanks to the onerous effort made by Mr. Manchanda.

Mr. Manchanda spends 3-4 hours every day writing public grievances/complaints/suggestions, because the passion to use pen-power against corruption is his only hobby. This also means taking out time of his normal routine schedule to attend hearings at Central Information Commission, Courts and members of public organized by educational institutions, RWAs (Resident Welfare Association) and NGOs (Non-Governmental Organisations). He has not only filed complaints/RTI-petitions to pull up public authorities for their wrong doings but has also filed many public-grievances with the CMO (Chief Medical Officer), PMO (Prime Minister Officer), Department of Administrative Reforms & Public Grievance and Public Interest Litigation (PIL) in High Court of Delhi after obtaining desired information under RTI Act.

Some of his key achievements are as follows:

Many government departments and public authorities implemented suitable reforms after irregularities and malpractices were exposed through his complaints and RTI-petitions, fixing responsibilities on concerned departments and ministries on various matters. On 01.10.2015 (International Day of Older Persons), the Hon'ble Chief Minister of Delhi honoured him as one of the best senior citizens doing social service for the care and welfare of elderly people.

He has written many articles on the use of RTI Act which has gained attention of concerned ones, and has also been highlighted in media as well as on the Govt. websites. In one of its judgments dated 9th January 2015, the Hon'ble Information Commissioner observed his petition to curb black money in immovable properties as one of the best RTI applications in the interest of fulfilling the objectives of the Right to Information Act.

When he came to know that hospitals were making huge profits from selling cardiac stents, the device to treat blockage/s in the heart, at a price much more than the import price, he filed many complaints, RTIs and appeal to CIC which finally led to the Govt./National Pharmaceutical Pricing Authority (NPPA) to cap the prices of stents to 1/5th the cost charged by hospitals. According to the CIC decision dated 22 Feb. 2017, his success will help so many unfortunate citizens whose loved ones are in need of a cardiac stent but are not able to bear the exaggerated price. The Commission finally appreciated the applicant, S.P. Manchanda, for having espoused a cause of larger public interest.

He filed many complaints/grievances and RTIs on the issue of high MRP of oncology medicines. Serious issues such as reducing the price of cancer medicines and generic medicines were heard by the Central Information Commission. CIC advised the Ministry of Health & Family Welfare and the Department of Pharmaceutical NPPA to check the menace of overpricing of drugs and make effective combined efforts to address this issue. Finally, the MRP of 390 non-scheduled cancer medicines were reduced by up to 87 percent, which would result in annual savings of Rs.800 crore for the patients (Economic Times 08.03.2019).

Presently, Mr. Manchanda is the Vice-President of Elderly People's Forum, Keshav Puram Delhi having more than 800 members on its roll. Elderly People Forum is not merely an organisation for him; it is the only path for him, blessed by God to serve other fellow elderly brothers and sisters by providing useful/ meaningful information from time-to-time, though in a small way as permitted by limited time and resources. He is also President and Convener-Trustee of a registered non-government organisation, Prakash-India, established with the aim of consumer awareness, environment protection and combating corruption in India. He is also associated with Transparency

International (India) and Akhil Bhartiya Grahak Panchayat, working for consumer protection in India. He has been a source of inspiration for the senior citizens who have sufficient experience and the willingness to devote time to write complaints and RTI-applications and use them as a tool to reduce corruption and remove red-tapism in public functioning in India. Further, he is motivating people, his fellow senior citizens in particular, to learn and use digital technology for active ageing and ageing gracefully, with full dignity and enjoyment.

Overwhelmed by the widespread publicity of his first book on anti-corruption, 'Embrace Your Own Power to Fight Corruption', the author, after understanding the need of digital awareness for senior citizens, has dealt with many important aspects of digital knowledge in this book. He has explained beautifully the different types of computers, mobile phones, social networking, online banking for their convenience and some important Apps for senior citizens for their well-being and hassle-free living. Further, the author has also dealt in detail with digital wellness and cyber security to prevent the risk associated with the use of computers and cell-phones in their day-to-day life. As more and more seniors are becoming digitally savvy, there is a need to explain to them how to be safe online.

–Publisher

ACKNOWLEDGEMENTS

This world is a better place for those who are always ready to show a positive direction to others and share their experience with the world. With this inspiring spirit, I started writing this book. Today, I am able to see my dream coming true, and for this I am grateful to everyone who contributed to this book.

First and foremost, I praise and thank God, the Almighty, for His showers of blessings throughout my work to complete the book positively and successfully.

Writing a book is harder than I thought and more rewarding than I could have ever imagined. It would not have been possible without the help of my dear friends, Mr. Satish Kumar Bahl (Former secretary to the Chief Editor – Hindustan Times) and Mr. Praneet Yadav (Digital Marketing Expert). I would like to express my deep and sincere gratitude to them. They were as indispensable and important to this book as I was.

Having an idea and turning it into a book is as hard as it sounds. The experience of writing and editing is both challenging and rewarding. I especially want to thank Mrs. Versha Manku

Acknowledgements

who helped me make this happen, and for the keen interest shown to complete this successfully in a short span of time. I would also like to thank her for her friendship, empathy, and editing of my entire book. Thank you so much Vershaji!

I am extending my heart-felt thanks to my family, my son Ankit, my daughter Deepika and her husband Anurag for their acceptance and patience during the discussion I had with them while working on this book.

Thanks to everyone on the Gullybaba team who helped and inspired me so much. Special thanks to Mr. Dinesh Verma, the Publishing Houseowner and CMD, and his entire team for the greatest cover designer I could have ever imagined.

I sincerely express gratitude to all the managing committee members of the Elderly People Forum. I have had the opportunity to work together for the welfare and empowerment of elderly members of our Forum; I want to say thanks to the respected colleagues for being the inspiration and motivating me in the project.

Finally, my thanks go to all those people who have supported me to complete the book directly or indirectly. They all kept me going on, and this book would not have been possible without their motivation and blessings.

–S.P. Manchanda

PURPOSE OF WRITING THIS BOOK

Digital technology today is a boon for the elderly people. Right from providing independence, connectivity to keeping your body and mind active, digital literacy has blessed silvers in many ways. But only a few senior citizens in India hook to the internet, social media and video chat to keep them socially engaged; get most of their daily activities done with the mere push of a button, engage in video games to keep their body and minds moving, manage their medication via Smartphone Apps, etc. However, there are ample online tools available to simplify the process of maintaining & accessing health information that can aid senior citizens in their day-to-day life.

Being digitally literate is as important as being literate. Through this book, the author wants to reach out to those people of the old generation, who are interested to know about the ways of using modern electronic equipment. The author wants to state that unlike what most senior citizens of today think, the use of modern gadgets is not tough. All that we need is practice and continuous use.

Even today, if we talk about digital literacy in our country, a large section is not digitally literate. This problem is not because that class is not aware of it, nor does this problem persist because that class does not want to learn it. But, this problem is increasing because that class has developed its own mindset. We are talking about nobody else but our senior citizens of our country India. There is no doubt that senior citizens want to live life happily and in a better way. With the correct use of technology, they can spend life more easily and comfortably. It is necessary for senior citizens to know what digital literacy is, and how to achieve it.

After the immense advancement of science in the modern era, many types of equipment exist among us today to provide more and more facilities to the common life, and to make the work of the houses easier. The youth are using these tools in their day-to-day life in a better way. It is often found that older people shy away from using modern-age appliances like Smartphones, tablets, computers, laptops, etc. due to which they find themselves lagging behind in this technology dominated era.

The basic purpose of this book is to digitally literate the elderly people and become aware of it. Based on my life experience, I know very well that it is very important to be digitally literate in present times. It is a fact that in the coming time, a person who will not be digitally literate, 3 will find himself in a way, different from a lot of parts of the world. You have no need to panic even if you have not been interviewed by the digital world yet. Being digitally literate is very simple; all that you need is a continuous practice.

Nothing is impossible in life; who can know this better than you as a senior citizen! You have crossed all the obstacles of your life and today you are able to spend your life in a joyful way. You can make this life more relaxed as well as purposeful. I propose a book with the aim of understanding the needs of older adults in gaining greater digital literacy.

It is my desire to empower senior citizens digitally, so first I would like to focus on what their goals are for digital use, areas where the digital activity is socially meaningful, and contributes directly to the development of meaning and identity.

The older population faces some specific challenges in using technology. Through this book, I will be trying to teach them on the various topics on the subject so that they all could deal with all problems arising due to lack of digital awareness.

The intention of writing this book is to teach the elderly people, who want to learn about modern equipment and technology. Through this book, I want to spread the awareness, skills, understandings, and reflective approaches necessary for an individual to operate devices comfortably.

Whether you want to learn how to use email, browse the Internet, make video calls with your grandkids, purchase gifts or other items online, or share and view photos with friends and family on Facebook, it is much easier than you think.

This book presents digital literacy in very simple ways. I hope that through this book you will be attracted to the digital world and try to make yourself digitally literate. I humbly believe that this book will help you learn much more about social networking and the digital world. Older persons are marginalized due to a lack of digital awareness. This book will surely help them in leading a more active and meaningful life with dignity.

It is usually not easy to convince the aged population to start using a Smartphone for ease, convenience, accessibility as well as for their safety. There are so many senior-friendly phones available, and many seniors still prefer to use non touch feature-phones. I would request the youth; if your senior loved one does not already have a Smartphone, now it would be a great time to talk to him/her about getting one and also about internet safety for seniors. Instead of purchasing one online, it would be preferable to take your loved elder one to the store so that he/she gets the opportunity to look at and play with a variety of different phones and see on his/her own as to what type would work best for him/her. While at the store, ask a salesman about Smartphones designed specifically for senior citizens. For example, GreatCall has a phone called the Jitterbug Smart which features a simplified menu for easy access to frequently used features such as the phone, text messages, email, Internet, camera, and pictures. It also features built-in Apps that provide instant access to emergency help, if needed. Additionally, Samsung Galaxy phones have an "easy mode" which converts the phone to a simpler mode of operation with larger icons.

Lastly, I would say that the greatest way to learn anything is by making mistakes. So, if you install too many Apps and make the memory run out, or if you take a while figuring out how a device works, don't panic. It happens to every first time user and several subsequent users too!

–S.P. Manchanda

Chapter 1

DIGITAL LITERACY: AN INTRODUCTION

Literacy refers to the skills of reading and writing words. A person who can read and write any language is called literate. Similarly, 'Digital literacy' means understanding and using the information available in a digital (electronic) form and if someone is able to do such things easily is called digitally literate. Digital literacy involves using technology, modern equipment and the internet. Learning to use technology is essential for achieving digital literacy and it is also important to get information on new topics of skill in view of the constantly changing era. The process of finding and reading a post on Google, watching your favourite videos on YouTube, downloading Apps to perform specific tasks and uploading your own posts or videos to the Internet is called digital literacy. With the help of digital literacy, we can know how to use technology, navigate and communicate through digital environments. Digital literacy not only provides you with better facilities but also connects you to the people and the technical facilities of the world.

Digital literacy means being able to do anything on the Internet according to your choice, to connect with your friends and loved ones, write a blog or post on the Internet, understanding the various applications and websites and being able to use it. It also ensures you that the actions you do on the Internet are neither illegal nor are you being part of any illegal activity. Digital literacy prepares you to use all these things, as well as you to deal with the frauds or troubles caused by it. Mainly hackers, spammers target those people who are not aware of the basics of the Internet or carelessly use the information spread on the Internet.

In this changing world, the Internet is used in a very advanced way. The Internet is usually found in all devices; this is the reason that along with technological devices like mobiles, laptops, etc., the Internet has also created a different place among us. With the help of the internet almost all the work is possible. We can accomplish our everyday tasks by being digitally literate, like buying any goods online, courier goods, business, money transfer, sharing our experience/work-skills with the rest of the world, contacting relatives, making video calls or audio calls, etc. With the help of this, today we can do shopping from home, buy medicines, even buy vegetables. Due to its advanced method, today we can also transfer money in a safe manner. To take advantage of all these facilities, it is necessary to know about the information of the Internet and ways to use it. This is the reason why today it has become extremely important for us 9 to be digitally literate.

In this digital world, senior citizens can be easily surprised by new equipment and knowledge around them. Presently they are surrounded by digital devices, whether it's Smartphones, social media, tablets, banking machines, or laptops. Since they cannot avoid using new technology, they should attempt to learn how to use all these technological advances to make life easier and comfortable. It becomes somewhat easy to become digitally literate when someone tries to learn more about the equipment and technology around him. More importantly, getting some simple training in using computers, tablets, and Smartphones can certainly help senior citizens stay connected with their families and friends. This is especially significant for senior citizens who wish to live alone and believe in ageing gracefully at home.

Today we are living in a highly technological age, and a substantial part of the change that we see around us is to do with the Internet and Social Media. Even though many older people from the earlier generation are reluctant, they are almost forced to adopt a few of these technologies and Social Media platforms, so that they can be comfortable in touch with their friends and family. In short, we can say that digital literacy allows people to work with computers and mobile devices, communicate online, use the internet safely, evaluate online resources, use software and hardware and be able to research online. Its ability to use technology and technological tools also helps senior citizens understand how it works to make life easier and comfortable.

Chapter 2

UNDERSTANDING COMPUTERS

The computer is a digital electronic system that manipulates information or data and performs complex calculations or otherwise processes data based on instructions in the form of stored programs and input data. Simply put, a computer is any device that accepts input from a user, performs calculations on that input, and provides desired output to the user.

A computer comes in three basic forms - desktop, laptop and tablet, but we include Smartphones as a fourth type of computer because of their personal computing capabilities.

The best way to learn about and become comfortable with computers is to start with the basics. Important parts of a computer that one should know include the computer case, the Central Processing Unit (CPU), the memory or RAM, the monitor, the keyboard, the mouse, and the printer.

The computer case, also called a computer chassis, or cabinet, is an enclosure that contains most of the components of a personal computer such as motherboard, hard drive, etc. except for display, keyboard, mouse, and printer.

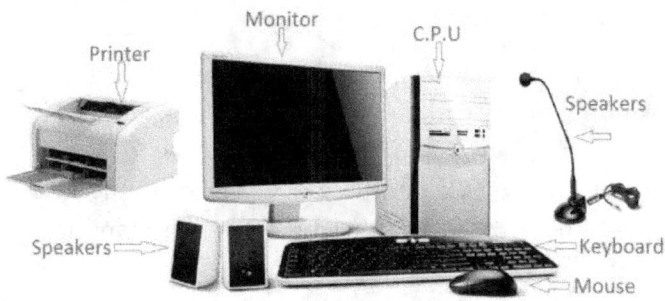

Basic parts of a Computer

The Central Processing Unit or CPU can be described as the computer's brain or core. It is located on something called the motherboard, which is inside the case. The case holds and protects the parts that enable the computer to function. It is also where one will generally find the power button that turns the machine on and off. A CPU is a chip that processes the information that the computer receives.

The RAM, or Random Access Memory, is the main memory of a computer, and it can affect the performance of a computer. In most computers, more RAMs can be added.

The monitor often resembles television. A computer monitor or computer screen is an output device that shows pictures for computers. The main difference between a monitor and a television is that a monitor does not have a television tuner to change channels. The high performance resolution of the monitor makes it easier to see lowercase letters and better graphics when compared to television. The monitor has a screen that shows the user text and images associated with the actions of the user and programs that are being run. It is connected to the computer along with the keyboard and mouse. Both the keyboard and the mouse enable the user to communicate and operate the computer.

Keyboard & Mouse: Most interactions with a computer involve using a keyboard and/or a mouse. The keyboard allows the user to type letters and numbers, while the user moves the mouse on a flat surface and presses its button (called clicking) after positioning the cursor thereby controlling movements on the computer screen. The mouse is thus an input device that is used to select and execute objects on a computer screen. You need to get familiar with the basic skills needed to tell a computer what to do or share information with others online.

A printer is an output device that prints paper documents. This includes text documents, images, or a combination of both. The two most common types of printers are inkjet Understanding Computers and laser printers. Inkjet printers are commonly used by consumers, while laser printers are a classic choice for businesses.

One of the primary uses of computers for most people is to access the Internet. The Internet, sometimes simply called Net, is a worldwide system of networks in which users at any one computer can, if they have permission, get information from any other computer (and sometimes talk directly to users at other computers). For this one will need a modem. Modem (modulator-demodulator) is a device that makes it possible for computers to communicate with one another without being directly connected to each other. A modem is typically used to send digital data over a telephone line or cable connection. The sending modem modulates the data into a signal that is compatible with the phone line and the receiving modem demodulates the signal back into digital data. A router can also be a good idea, as this device can provide an added layer of security for your Internet connection. A wireless router will be needed to go online using a tablet or laptop computer; a wired one will work fine if you only have a desktop computer. The difference between a modem and a router is that a modem connects your home to the internet, while a router creates the network inside your house. It is easy to get the two devices mixed up if your Internet Service Provider (ISP) rents both to you as part of an internet package. Service from an Internet service provider is also required to use the Internet. These services vary and are available with different speeds that can affect things such as how quickly a Web page loads and the quality of streaming movies. One should consider how important speed is to them, as faster speeds are often available at higher prices. A Web browser is a software that allows one to access the Web page. The browser software will need to be used to connect to a search engine if the user wants to search for information online. Let us be familiar with different types of computers.

Types of Computers

Computers in the 70s and 80s were large, heavy, intimidating machines that were not very useful outside of the specific tasks programmed to execute. But, with the advancement of science, the size of computers is also getting smaller. A laptop has replaced the huge desktop in nearly every household. A tablet, or tablet PC, is a portable computer that uses a touchscreen as its primary input device. A Smartphone is a cellular telephone with an integrated computer into one unit. Let us take a look at different types of computers.

Desktop

A desktop computer is a personal computer designed for regular use at a single location on or near a desk or table due to its big size and power requirements. It includes a screen called a monitor, a mouse, a keyboard, and the Central Processing Unit (CPU). Many newer versions of desktop computers,  known as "all-in-ones," combine the monitor and CPU into a single unit with a separate keyboard and mouse.

Laptop

A laptop computer is a small personal computer. They are designed to be more portable than traditional desktop computers, with many of the same abilities. Laptops are able to be folded flat  for transportation and have a built-in keyboard and touchpad. A laptop computer is smaller than a desktop computer, generally less than three inches thick. In addition to the power cable it also uses Understanding Computers battery power, which can last for several hours.

Tablet

Tablet Computer is defined as a flat, thin mobile computer that comes fitted with a touchscreen display and a rechargeable battery. Over the past few years, tablet PCs

have become so popular due to their great features, specialized Apps and portability. Tablets vary by operating system and processors. Apple and Intel manufacture the most widely used processors for tablets. Some tablets use Android OS, others Windows OS while iPad tablets from Apple rely on iOS. Tablet computers resemble Smartphones in some ways and can also be used to take photos, make phone calls, send messages, record videos and perform other tasks that can be performed by a Smartphone as well.

Smartphone

When the internet becomes enabled in a normal cell-phone and we can do many things using it, then such a cellphone is called a Smartphone. Similar to a tablet, there is a touchscreen surface and has cameras for photography and video recording. Smartphones can be used by us in both as a consumer and a business context, and are now almost integral to everyday modern life. Many seniors use  their Smartphones to engage with friends and family members.

General Computer Help

Computers, like cars and other machines, can face problems with reduced performance and can even break down. These issues can occur in the computer's hardware, such as when a mouse stops functioning or the hard drive fails, or software, like when a video file becomes unreadable.

Computers may also slow down dramatically, freeze up and stop functioning, or have problems connecting to the Internet.

When these things happen, it will be necessary for the user to seek help to diagnose and repair the computer. Elderly users can benefit from online or classroom computer training that teaches them how computers work and how to fix minor problems when they arise, as well as perform maintenance tasks to prevent issues from happening in the first place.

Computer security is also an important issue for users to be aware of, especially for seniors, who are often a specific target of certain types of online scams. A general rule to follow on the Internet is if an offer is presented that seems too good to be true, it generally is a scam. It is important to install antivirus software to protect the computer from malware.

A firewall is also needed to protect personal information. It is also necessary to keep both types of software up-to-date with the latest patches to keep the computer immunized from digital infections. Also, never volunteer personal information over email, chat, or other methods of communication except to trusted friends or family.

What computer does?

As we have now come to know that there are different types of computers; like desktop, laptop, tablet and especially Smartphone (small and compact computers), it is all in the form of computers. Now we will discuss what the computer does.

A computer is a machine or device that processes, calculates and performs operations based on the instructions given by the software program. It is designed to execute applications and provides various solutions by combining hardware and software components. But moving towards practicality, it is much more than that.

In the modern era, computers have become an important part of our daily lives. Along with this, the use of computers has increased a lot during the last few years. The invention of computers symbolizes the advancement of technology in mankind. Further, the computer has made our life easier. If the computer had not been invented, we would not have made much progress today and our life would not have been easy. It could be one of the most resourceful inventions ever made. It can be your friend in solitude, entertaining you. It can enlighten you with all knowledge available on the internet.

It is generally felt that older people are uncomfortable with new forms of technology and they feel more hesitant to use computers than younger people. Another misconception is that the elderly are unable to learn new skills. When technology training opportunities are provided, very few opportunities are usually given to elderly people for training.

Elderly people who learn these devices and techniques usually do not have problems at all using these things. It also must be mentioned that some of the devices that appear to be fearful, it is known that most of these devices aid a person during daily work, but it is thought that computers such as Smartphones are capable of revealing information that is naturally undesired. The result is that there is considerable confusion over the safety though the world is largely turning to this facility that is both time saving as well as convenient. Elderly people need to know all that is out there in order for them to feel comfortable using the computers. Once this is done, the computers are not difficult tools to utilize, and elderly people may communicate easily with people and organisations in any part of the world. First of all, to get out of all this confusion and fear, it will be necessary for us to know what it can do for us, so that we can use it to improve our lives.

Computers are used at home for work and entertainment purposes, at offices, in hospitals, in government organizations. Here, we are going to discuss some of the uses of computers at home:

Home Budget

Computers can be used to control the home budget. You can easily calculate your income and expenses by a computer. You can apply any calculation on these columns to plan your household budget by listing all expenses in one column and income in another column. There are also specialist software that can easily show your income and expenses and generate good reports for you. Understanding Computers 20 Digital Literacy for Senior Citizens Once you come to know about the various expenses, you can check which expenses are extravagant and curb accordingly.

Games

 We can use the computer at our home to play games. Nowadays different types of computer games are available in the market. These games are a source of amusement and entertainment. Many games are also available which are especially developed to improve your mental ability and thought power.

Working from Home

Today people can manage the office work at home. The owner of a company can check the work of the employees working from home. The employee can control his office while sitting at home. During lockdown, most of the employees were working from home using computers.

Entertainment

People can find entertainment on the internet. They can listen to songs, watch videos and movies and download songs and videos to watch. They can also watch live programs and matches on the internet.

Information

People can find any type of information on the internet. Educational and informative websites are available to download books, tutorials, etc. to improve their knowledge and learn new things.

Chatting & Social Media

You can chat with friends and family on the internet using different software like Skype, WhatsApp, Telegram, E-mail etc. Also, you can have a conversation with your relatives and friends anytime on social media websites like Facebook, Twitter and Google Plus. Further, you can also share photos and videos with relatives & friends.

Importance of technology in elderly life

It is well understood that using computers with new technology is essential in our lives and you will come to know that to learn it only requires some practice. So, now you need to express a desire to learn it. The simplest way to learn this is to first try to make sure according to your need, what you want to do in your life through this technology. It will become quite easy to learn after determining this. After doing this, you will be able to use different computers and technology better, according to your need, and can also use it daily.

The computers or mobile phones make your life a lot easier and bring the world at your seat to absorb information and to put these to your best use. Almost anything can be accessed through your computer, from your bank account to your favourite restaurant. If you use it well, life can be a lot easier.

Whether the person is a senior citizen, who is considering the need to learn more about computers, or a person who wants to teach an elder member of the family how to use computers, it is significant to first understand how computers are useful for you. Frequent use of computers can help improve a person's mental agility, build confidence, and create a sense of independence. Computers can make life more convenient by giving the elderly a way to read the latest news, research health issues, pay bills online, and manage their finances. For people who may live in another city, state, or even country than their grandchildren or children, it allows them to communicate by email, chat, or video conference. Keep in mind that when mobility or health is an issue, computers are very beneficial for the people to connect them socially with each other.

We already accept that computers are an invaluable part of modern society that has become as standard as cars.

However, it is difficult to find a home or business that does not have some type of computer, where some people still do not use computers or find it difficult to use them. It is often the senior citizens who are still uncomfortable learning this new technique.

Now that we have established why computers are important in today's world, and you understand what the main types of computer are; it is time to get digitally literate with the wonderful ways you can use them.

It may sound fancy and unrealistic to some, but it is not that hard to become technically aware seniors. Just try and keep an open mind and let go of any preconceived notions that technology is complicated and not 'your thing'.

It is true that most of your lives were lived without the modern gadgets of today, and if you are not well aware of technology, yet that does not mean you cannot use technology. Now just give it a chance, then you will know for yourself what technology can do for you.

It is nice to know that you can stay connected to loved ones and friends (no matter if you or they are in the grocery store, traveling abroad on vacation, or even in the yard gardening).

While it is one of the most important things of the 21st century, the internet is largely (and wrongly) considered as a young person's tool. Encouraging older generations to learn basic computer skills can be somewhat difficult, but not too problematic.

After the practice and learning how to use a mouse and keyboard, you will find that staying in contact with family members has never been so easy. You can even order your groceries, food online and have these all delivered to your home with just a few clicks of the mouse. Further there are also Apps (applications) to keep your brain active.

Way to get information

Our modern life has become easier and for this the people of the world should thank the huge contribution of Internet technology for communication and information sharing. There is no doubt now that the Internet has made our lives a lot easier and more convenient. We can use the Internet now to communicate with people around the world, search for information and for study. Apart from this, we can make new friends using the Internet, get to know different cultures and explore new businesses.

The Internet not only allows us to communicate via email, but also ensures easy availability of information, images, videos and products, among other things. Every new day, the Internet continues to offer a new feature, something new that is very attractive and convenient and that makes lives much easier for web users. Yet, there are some unwanted elements or disadvantages in the Internet as explained hereafter.

People can use the facilities and information whenever and wherever they want. As far as searching for things on the internet is concerned, many people do not even know Understanding Computers the appropriate way to do it. First of all, try to understand your device before surfing the internet. Your device is a tool from which you can use the internet but before searching anything, try to learn the basic function of the device you are going to use. Because when you will not learn how to operate your device, you cannot use the internet in a better way. It is only with the help of your device, that you can easily get information and use the internet in the best way. Let's learn more about the Internet and their uses.

Here are some of the best resources available to senior citizens who want to know their way around computers.

Google is the foremost Internet search engine; Google.com is the most visited website in the world. Its primary service is offering consumer-targeted online search for things anywhere at any time.

Whether you want to learn any recipe, read any book online, find a path, want to know about any celebrity, local and world news and anything that is in your mind; Google will help to search almost all content according to your command. This will help you entertain yourself. With this help you can search anything, learn from it and download it.

How to search on Google?

To search any topics, you have to open Google Chrome or visit www.google.com and then the search bar will open on screen. In that search bar you can type the topic of your search, such as best doctors in your vicinity, recreation parks near your house, old age homes in your city, food court etc. as per your need.

Q Search Google or type a URL

Few tips and tricks to find your desired information on Google

Always start with a simple search like "where is the closest bank to me." You may also add a few descriptive words if necessary. For your convenience, few tips are given below:

1. If you are looking for a place or product in a specific location, add the location. For example, type, "Shopping Mall, Rajouri Garden".

2. If you find difficulty in typing, you may search with your voice, say "Ok Google" or select the Microphone icon. Speak clearly whatever you want to search and the result will be on your screen within no time.

3. Choose your words carefully. When you are deciding which words to enter in the search box, try to choose the words that are more likely to appear on the site you want to search. For example, instead of typing where my money is, type in the name of your bank, which Google will inform you by searching!

4. While searching do not worry about little things like spellings. Google's spell-checker routinely uses the most common spelling of the typed word, whether you spelled correctly or not.

Let's see some search examples to find quick and accurate results:

Dictionary: Enter 'definition' with any word to know the definition of that word.

Weather: Type 'weather' to see the weather in your location or add a city name, like "weather Mumbai", to see the weather for a certain place.

Unit Conversation: Enter any conversion; say 150 dollars in rupees to get a result.

Sports: Search for the name of your team to find the schedule, game scores and anything else you desire.

Entertainment: Just type the name of a celebrity, location, movie, or song to search for the desired information.

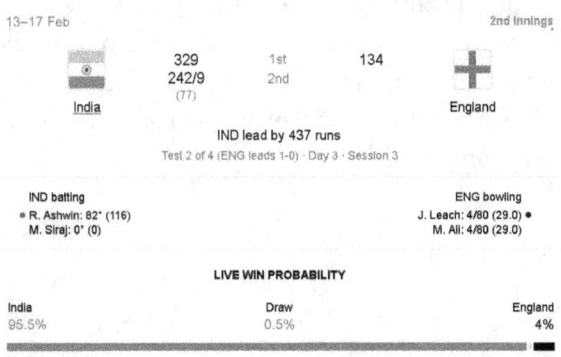

There are unlimited uses of Google, but some are given below:

1. You can watch pics, videos, movies, etc.

2. You can download various contents like photos, videos, songs, files, books, etc.

3. You can search for any information in many other languages other than English.

4. You can get a translation of your word or sentence/s in the desired language.

5. It is quite easy to search websites related to your topic.

6. Google provides the best result to its user according to his/her requirements.

You can take advantage of auto complete or Google suggest feature, it shows you the keywords from all the people searching in different regions. You can also learn online courses.

Usage Benefits for Senior Citizens

Study shows that computer games give balance benefits to senior citizens. A CBS News article explains that elderly adults can experience improvement in their ability to walk after playing games on a computer. Seniors, who use modern technology such as the Internet and mobile phones, have a reduced risk of social isolation. Further, seniors who play video games exhibit a better sense of emotional well-being.

Chapter 3

SMARTPHONE GUIDE FOR ELDERS

As an elder, you must have felt many times that you also need a cellphone or mobile phone so that you too stay connected with your loved ones and feel safe. The phone is the easiest way to stay connected to everyone in this time period. In the earlier times, phones were used only for making calls and sending messages, but today with the help of technology, it has given a new form. Now, these Smartphones have been made advanced, which can not only make calls for you but can also do many other types of tasks, such as video calls, games, taking videos and photos, shopping, payment, etc. Just understand that it is not just a phone but an assistant who is able to do all the tasks related to your daily routine and will also help you in doing all the tasks. There are mainly three types of mobile phones.

Basic phones can make voice calls, send and receive SMS (Short Message Service) messages. Such basic phones also permit users to easily create notes, set an alarm, and use as a calculator. But such phones do not offer advanced features like internet connectivity, camera and map. They can be purchased at a low-cost price.

Feature phones incorporate features additional to basic phones such as increased storage and the ability to access the Internet but lack the advanced functionality of a Smartphone. Most present-day feature phones are flip phones, which feature a phone and dialing pad that can be opened with the flip of a hand. They generally use physical buttons rather than touch screens.

Smartphones offer advanced capabilities and features over feature phones, are more like computers with Operating Systems (OS) installed in them, allowing users to add applications (Apps) to their phones. Let us discuss some advanced features of Smartphone:

If you have to buy something, you can take help from your Smartphone. If you have to find a way/path to get somewhere, you can get a map on the Smartphone; this mobile phone will help you even if you have to pay money for your water bill, electricity bill, TV bill (Airtel, Tata Sky, etc.) and other types of services. If you want to keep some of your memorable moments through photos or videos, then the mobile phone will act as a camera for you. Calendars, calculators, clock, music, etc. have come in your hands with advanced facilities.

The thing to think about is, all this is possible through Smartphones, and it also makes our daily routine work easier as well as being with us as an assistant. Why are most of the elderly people still not accepting these facilities? The fact is that in today's technological era, most of the elders believe that the use of technology is a very complicated process and difficult too.

Let us start with an example; have you ever noticed that even small children of today know how to operate mobile phones? Are they taught to use all this? How can they easily use mobile at such a young age? This is not surprising, but there is a simple answer. Children simply use mobiles very passionately and by using them daily, they get used to operating mobiles. Children easily listen to their favourite songs on mobile phones, watch videos, play games, and do other favourite things. Using Smartphones after continuous use is not a big deal for them.

It is a fact; the easiest way to learn any device is to use that device on a regular basis. Find a reason and use it continuously. After continuous use of the device, you may soon be able to use it properly.

No doubt, these days many elderly use their Smartphones for nearly everything. Here are a few common uses of Smartphones for seniors:

- Making emergency phone calls
- Photography, Videography
- Video chatting with grandchildren
- Texting with friends and relatives
- Using GPS to help navigate when driving or walking
- Checking the weather

- Monitoring health and medicine time through Apps
- Accessing the internet for knowledge
- Play games

Interestingly, you can also connect your Smartphone to your TV and enjoy your content the way you want. The wireless technology is improving and evolving day by day around us to wirelessly connect our Smartphones to TV. It is always a great idea to stream YouTube on Netflix video from smartphone to television as it is more comfortable with content on bigger screens. Smartphone mirroring to TV is very useful in the meeting room and classrooms, because these are the places where meetings and presentations are more often. In order to mirror smartphone screen onto television, the criteria required is both your smartphone and TV must support Miracast. It is quiteeasy to connect the two for screen sharing by following these steps:

1. **WiFi network:** Please ensure that your phone and TV are connected to the same Wi-Fi network.

2. **TV settings:** Go to the input menu on your TV and turn on "screen mirroring"

3. **Mobile settings:** Look for screen mirroring/cast screen/ wireless display option on Smartphone and tap to turn on. By clicking on this option, your mobile identifies the Miracast enabled TV or dongle and displays it on the screen;for example, LG, Samsung, etc.

4. **Select TV:** Select your TV from the list of devices. Tab on the name to initiate connection. If the connection is successful then you can mirror the content from your phone to television.

5. **Establish connection:** Follow the on-screen instructions to complete the setup. This is sometimes required

entering a code displayed on your TV into your smartphone to establish a connection. To stop mirroring tap on disconnect.

With screen mirroring one can watch on mirror varied content without worrying about the compatibility. You can send a presentation onto TV from your smartphone, play games on your smartphone and stream it on a bigger screen and even browse the web from mobile and mirror the screen.

Chapter 4

SOCIAL NETWORKING

We humans are social creatures. Most of us live with families, work in communities, and identify as a member of a culture and nation. From the moment we are born, we connect with others. So maybe it is no surprise that our relationships with others continue to play an important role late into our lives. Numerous health studies have shown that, if we want to live better as we progress deep into life, we should seek out and maintain a good social network. Growing older does not mean leading lesser than a full life. Aging adults can improve their well-being by maintaining strong social networks.

A social network is your network of social interactions and relationships. It does not matter if this person is an old friend, a colleague, a family member, or just someone you always run into at the park; if you enjoy their company and conversation, they are part of your social network.

Often, there is a strong perception in the minds of people that social media like Facebook, Twitter, Instagram, YouTube, and Pinterest are only meant for the younger crowd. It is the young who are always on the mobile-phone, updating their details and posting selfies, as we see it. A recent statistic about Indian Facebook users suggests that there are 0.6 million females and 1.8 million male Facebook users in the age group of 65 years and above. When you compare it with the 18 to 24 years age group, it shows 23.4 and 73.8 respectively for females and males. In another platform Instagram, the 55+ users account for just 1 percent of its 43 million users. So, if you go by statistics, the perceptions seem to be true.

But then, we have also seen that there are many disruptors and path-breaking seniors, who are changing the scenarios. We have learned about a few seniors who have garnered millions of followers on YouTube, and also on Facebook. These people were introduced to these platforms by their family or friends and had quickly learned to use these platforms as a way of engaging with the society. And it is not just the older generation that follows these people, but also the younger generation.

Today, social media has changed the way we intermingle with the world around us. From connecting with old friends to organizing community gatherings, social media has brought the world to a small place, bringing many generations together on one platform. With nearly 60 percent of adults over the age of 65 online and 45 percent of those on at least one social network, it will not be out of place to say that social media is impacting the lives of seniors in an unparalleled way.

Social media platforms, especially Facebook, can greatly help senior citizens find their old companions and make new friends with people of the same age group with similar interests.

Likewise, it can be very interesting to find long lost friends and restart those meaningful friendships. If you are an aging adult, stay active and do not shy away from WhatsApp, Facebook, Gmail and online learning.

Social media is entertaining too. Whether it is laughing at a meme, catching up with old friends, reliving the past through clips of old shows, playing games, or reading articles, social media is a great way to laugh, learn, and share.

Online social media is very useful, Facebook being one of them. It is a globally famous social networking website. Due to its popularity, many works have been done to secure users' data in it. Every effort has been made to make it quite safe and easy for the users.

Along with social networking sites, you can also use Twitter to connect with people. Twitter is an online news and social networking site. Further, LinkedIn is a social network specifically designed for career and business professionals to connect. Let us understand and discuss all these four, Facebook, Twitter, LinkedIn and Instagram with some details in the following pages.

Facebook

Facebook is a social network website (App is also available in play store) that allows users, who sign-up for free profiles, to connect with relatives, friends, colleagues or anonymous people online. It helps users to share pictures, videos and articles, as well as to convey their own thoughts and ideas to as many people they like. With nearly 2.8 billion monthly active users as of the fourth quarter of 2020, Facebook is the biggest social network worldwide.

Facebook was launched on 4th February 2004 by Mark Zuckerberg with Harvard college students. The Facebook service can be accessed by a large range of devices with Internet connectivity, such as personal computers, tablets and Smartphones. Now, connecting with friends and family is faster and easier than ever. You can share updates and photos, engage with friends and stay connected to communities important to you.

On Facebook, you can connect to the online world of Facebook by creating your ID (Identity). Creating an ID is very easy. You just have to provide some of your information; such as: your name, mobile number, date of birth, etc. Providing a mobile number is optional. After signing up, your ID is created on Facebook. You can login (proceed) to Facebook with your ID and password. You can find the ID of your friends, peers or any other Facebook user as per your wish, send them a friend request or you can accept the friend request received by them and keep them in your friends list. If someone accepts your friend request or you accept someone's friend request, then you will be friends with each other. You can see what social activities are done by them like photo share, post, comments, etc. through notifications and if you want, you can participate in that activity by reacting or making comments.

Facebook Company has tried to make it extremely easy for the users. The feature given in it is quite easy to use. Let's take a look at some of the features given in Facebook and see how it can work for us.

Features on the Facebook App include:

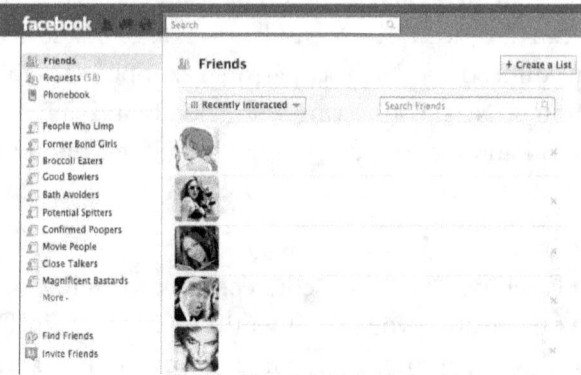

- **Connect with people:** It allows you to connect with your relatives, friends and meet new people around the world on this platform. It is a better medium to connect with people from all over the world, and understand their culture. On Facebook, you can make friends from different countries and interact with them. It is quite easy.

- **Set status:** You are free to set status updates & use Facebook emoji to help relay what's going on in your world. You can set pics and videos as status, and may post them on your page.

- **Share online:** People from all over the world share their photos, videos and activities here. If you want, you can use Facebook to share your photos, videos, and your favorite memories with your Facebook Friends.

- **Get notifications:** If any activity related to you on Facebook or any kind of activity is done by your friends, then you will get information about it by notification. After that, you can check that notification of your

Facebook by opening it and if you want you can join their activity. When friends like and comment on your posts you may react and comment if you feel to do so.

- **Find local social events:** Facebook provides an online platform where people give'information about their local events. You can find such events according to your wish. By getting information about that, you can participate in events with people and visit friends or make plans to meet up with friends.

- **Play games with any of your Facebook Friends:** Facebook App gives you a chance to connect with the world as well as play with people from all over the world. There are many games available, which you can play online with your Facebook Friends or any other Facebook user. And you can also enjoy different types of games as per your wish. It is easy to connect and play.

- **Backup:** The Facebook App is a very large online channel. Here, you can save your photos/videos as well as backup them and keep them separate by capturing them according to the album. From here, you will not be afraid of losing photos/videos, all photos/videos will be safe online. Further, you can also recover these by the backup process.

- **Follow your favorite:** As you already know, people from all over the world are connected on Facebook. Also, some celebrities get connected through Facebook by creating their online official pages, Such as film stars, political leaders, artists, Global businessmen or leaders, sports persons, social activists and many more. These types of famous people make their official page on Facebook to stay connected with the general public and their followers. You can use Facebook to follow your favourite celebrities, and get events related to their lives. Here, you can follow their official page to know about the events related to the life of famous people, as well as the latest news of famous companies, websites and businesses.

Look up local businesses

Facebook is used by most businesses for social media marketing. This is the easiest way for any business to reach as many people as possible. For this, here your company tells about itself, it also tells the timing and shares photos related to their business. You can use all these to get better knowledge, see reviews, operation hours, and pictures about the business.

Watch live videos on the go

 Facebook has added a new feature, Go Live, under which you can record live video through Facebook, and then the video that you are recording will be broadcast online. You can select the option in which you can choose the people you want to reach, whether you want it to your friends, followers or the world; can share with all. Live videos are also

used by celebrities. If you want, you can watch their live videos and stay connected with them.

The Facebook App helps you stay connected with your interests and like-minded friends. Sharing photos directly from your camera is very easy; you have complete control over your photos and privacy. You can choose when to keep individual photos private or even set up a secret photo album to control who will see it. Facebook helps you connect with the world's latest news and current events.

Facebook Messenger (generally known as Messenger) helps you stay close with those who matter most, from anywhere and on any device. Messenger is just like texting/chatting. Messenger is the best way to communicate with all the people and businesses in the world. Interestingly, you don't need a Facebook account to use Messenger. While the two are partially connected when you have a Facebook account, you are not required to have one to use Messenger (your phone number and name will suffice). You can upload and send photos, videos, start group chats, and use voice and video calling without ever having to sign up for a Facebook account.

Twitter

Twitter is an online news and social networking site where people speak in short messages called tweeting. Tweeting means posting short messages for someone who follows you on Twitter, hoping that your messages may be interesting and useful to your audience.

Twitter is a service for people to communicate and stay connected through the exchange of quick, frequent messages.

Twitter is a social website where people are allowed to make their posts about different topics. Twitter allows its users to keep their friends and family informed of their current status. Twitter first began in 2008 as a small project, but now it has more than two billion users worldwide.

You should know that Twitter is a social networking and micro-blogging service that allows you to post short text messages upto 280 characters in length, called tweets, to your friends, or followers and can include links to relevant websites and resources.

Twitter can have many uses for both personal and business. This is a great way to keep in touch with your relatives and friends and quickly disseminate information about where you are and what you are doing nowadays. "For example: I am enjoying the exhibitions at the World Trade Centre in Delhi, would anyone like to join me?"

If you are interested, you can track hundreds of favorite Twitter users and enjoy reading their content at a glance. This is ideal for our modern attention-deficit world. Twitter is the source for what's happening in the world. From local news to world news, entertainment to sports and cinema, from politics to Bollywood fun stories that go viral, when this happens anywhere in the world, it happens first on Twitter. You can find friends or follow influential people - every voice can influence this world. So, come and join this Twitter's world. You can join the conversation you wish to like.

Twitter is easy to use. You can tweet, re-tweet, reply to tweets, share or like if you want to do so. You may chat privately or go big and initiate a group conversation with anyone who follows you. Twitter is the best place to track your friends and other followers or to follow your favorite celebrity. Also engage your social network with hundreds of interesting Twitter users with remarkable links, photos and videos to read their content at a glance. Further, you can keep an eye on which of your tweets are liked or re-tweeted.

Twitter encourages you to find people you like and follow people who are interested in you. Maintaining a social connection has never been easier. Twitter allows celebrities to build a personal connection with their fans. This is the main reason that Twitter has now become the most used social media platform, not only in India but in the whole world.

You can also create your Twitter account in simple steps. To create the Twitter account, visit the Twitter website and Go to http://twitter.com and find the sign up box, or go directly to https://twitter.com/signup. You will be directed to enter the requested information such as your name and email address. You should provide your real name only as your username to help your friends find it conveniently. Once your account is created, you should login and then click on "Settings". From here, you can set up your account details, manage your password, register your mobile phone and IM account, configure how you receive Notices, upload your photo and customize your account's design.

You can create a great engaging profile, customize your profile, tweet a photo, description, location, and background photo. Further, you can post visual content and optimize your posting time. You can use '#' hash-tags in your tweets and draw in followers outside of Twitter.

You should know what is trending now. Discover top trending hash-tags and breaking news headlines. Whether you are interested in sports highlights, pop culture and entertainment or politics, Twitter is your source of information.

LinkedIn

LinkedIn is a social networking website specifically designed to connect career and business professionals. This is a network for people in professional jobs in which users can make connections with other people with whom they have worked, post their work experience and skills, look for suitable jobs, and look for workers for them.

If you want to use the social network for professional use, then it may be a better choice for you, here you can present yourself to the world in a professional manner. LinkedIn has more than 200 million members around the world who use LinkedIn to improve their careers and businesses.

Unlike any other social network in which you can be "friends" with someone, LinkedIn is about professional persons building planned relationships. As such, the number of connections is less important than the type of connections. As it is about quality and not the quantity of members in the case of LinkedIn, it stops showing a real number of connections, once you reach 500 members.

LinkedIn is a valuable resource for career and business professionals to network, obtain resources and support, and build relationships with potential customers, clients, and partners. It's ideal for home-based business owners, freelancers, and telecommuters, as it can help them build their business and career, as well as stay connected to the outside world.

You can start by connecting with those you know and who know you, and through them build a larger network for the purpose of gaining resources, finding freelance work or clients, and building alliances and partnerships. Although LinkedIn has its own platform and system different from other networks, learning to use LinkedIn is no more difficult than learning to use any other social networking site. You may learn to use it by creating a personal LinkedIn account and profile.

Here, you will not find anything like the rest of the social network websites. However, networking on LinkedIn is much different. You will not find members posting cat videos or pictures of what they made for dinner. LinkedIn, being a site for LinkedIn professionals as well as for freelance work, everything is scaled up to take care of careers and businesses. As you build your profile and seek out connections, endorsements, and recommendations, you will want to be professional.

To get started you need to create a LinkedIn login. Later on, you can also upgrade to one of the following paid LinkedIn subscriptions: Premium Career, Business Plus, LinkedIn Learning, Sales Navigator (three levels), and Recruiter Lite. Using just the basic free services is sufficient for many employees and home business owners and gets you features such as having a professional profile of skills, experiences, and lots more. It gives limited information about who has viewed your profile. You may upgrade to increase some of these features.

Once you sign up for a LinkedIn account, either free or paid, you can then create your own professional profile. You must remember that this is a professional-minded website, so it is very important that the information in your profile represents your business or career. Some of the items you can add to a profile include the basics of your resume, a summary of yourself, your contact information, links to your website or blog, your previous employers, published books, and notable projects. You should add a professional picture, as people are reluctant to connect with someone without a photo.

As your LinkedIn profile is like a resume or business card, it is basically a marketing tool. That is why you should consider writing a benefits-oriented profile so that potential partners can recognize the advantage of working with you.

As soon as your profile is complete, you can now publish it and start looking for 'connections'. A connection is a person that you know, or would like to know. Basically the idea is to create as many direct connections as you can by adding people within your own professional circle and further branching out to include their connections. Your connections can also provide introductions to other professionals you might be interested in meeting. Moreover, connections can also endorse you for skills and provide you with proper recommendations.

You can use LinkedIn to build a home business, it can help you to start and grow a home business. It provides you with an opportunity to communicate and collaborate with other professionals interested in sharing business and industry knowledge. It is an efficient tool for locating those who may contribute to the success of your business.

LinkedIn allows you to have an online resume and business card where potential clients, customers, and joint venture partners can learn about and connect with you. Get introductions to potential clients, customers, and colleagues and thereafter search available job postings placed on the LinkedIn website by members. While you can also search the web for jobs, through LinkedIn, the big benefit is that many job posts are exclusive to LinkedIn: They are not advertised anywhere else. Such postings often have a requirement that you have one or more LinkedIn recommendations. Further, there is a chance that someone within your LinkedIn network already works there or knows somebody who does, thus increasing your chances for an interview and selection.

Instagram

 Instagram is a social media platform, owned by Facebook, on which users can post photos, videos and stories from anywhere in the world, and then add captions, filters, hashtags, polls, question answers, gifs and so much more. Users can engage with each other, explore their interests, follow pages, talented individuals and celebrities they like and even grow their own business or website. This App can be downloaded for Android, iOS and Windows Mobile. It can also be accessed on Computers. In short, if your interest is sharing and watching photos/videos from each other's lives, it is a must have!

For installing Instagram on an Androidphone, tap the Play Store icon on the Home screen. Then tap the Search box at the top of the screen, and start typing the word Instagram. Thereafter tap the Instagram in the results list and tap Install. You can now open the Instagram.

Instagram is a social networking service that is hugely popular, especially among the young. It is a photo and video sharing network that is owned by Facebook. Users can upload pictures and videos with hashtags, location, and many filters to make them relevant for those who search for specific information. There are many influencers on Instagram. It has become so popular that many brands have their page and use it to reach out to the people. Also, if you have many followers, then your Instagram page will also become very valuable for advertisers.

So, while there is only a small percentage of seniors using this site, those few are good enough to create a wave and make the news. There are a few who have been introduced to this site and are using it to enrich their lives as well as that of others and also enjoying it.

So, do you have an interest that you are good at and would like to share it with the world out there and also keep yourself engaged? Then, perhaps it's time you checked out Instagram and started your own page. You just might become the next Instagram sensation who would inspire many others of your age to take up the same.

Facebook has 1.8 billion daily active users as compared to Instagram which has 500 million monthly active users. Images perform better on Instagram than Facebook since that's what Instagram is primarily used for. That is why text is mostly left to Facebook. Now, it's up to you how to use each social network.

CHAPTER 5

ONLINE COMMUNICATION

Online communication refers to the several ways (such as e-mail, social networking sites, etc.) in which individuals and computers can communicate with each other through a networked computer. Most people think about speech and sending letters when they think about communication but there are many other ways we can also use to communicate with each other. These ways include: E-mail (electronic mail), online chatting, etc. Yahoo, Gmail and Hotmail are not only top e-mail providers but also offer 'real-time' messaging, or instant messaging.

Technology has provided people with the means to do things that would otherwise be impossible. Now, that technology has given people around the world the ability to communicate among themselves, some believe that it has limited mutual interaction with those who are closest. Online communication via e-mail and instant messaging is far more effective than using the telephone or post office as it is possible to talk to multiple people simultaneously due to their fast speed. E-mail is even more widespread and influential because the people next door and people all over the world just keep in touch by sending emails to each other and even do extensive business.

In today's world, millions of people like to communicate online. Online communication is a very convenient way of communication and chatting to a person is very easy. E-mail and chat are modern convenient methods for communicating with the help of social media resources and most people consider this mode of communication as most suitable for them. The benefits of communication online are also visible; they include communication with relatives and friends who live in far-off places. In addition, communication online is a fast and convenient way of expressing your feelings, being in touch and being available for any news, opportunities, upcoming events or job offers.

E-mail

E-mail (electronic mail) has become one of today's standard means of communicating electronically. Electronic mail (email or e-mail) is a method of exchanging messages ("mail") between people using electronic devices.

In earlier times, we used to communicate with our loved ones through letters. Now the people, especially businesses, have adopted email as their general form of day-to-day communication mostly because of its speed. This makes email much more popular than traditional paper mail or letters as it is commonly known today. With letters, writers and recipients are forced to wait days to complete communication. Now, technically society has come very far.

The technology has developed so much that with its help you can send letters too, not by writing on paper but by typing electronically, such as SMS. Today, technology has provided the facility to send any type of mail in electronic form. If you want to send a letter to your loved ones, apply for a job, get a letter from someone; you can do all this work on your computer or smart mobile phone only. With the help of electronic mail, you can deliver your mail to the concerned person in seconds. The process is quite easy and safe also.

You must be somewhat cautious about how to use words in an email. The receiver does not have the opportunity to see the body language or hear the sender's voice to explain the meaning of the words. Self-written words can take on unexpected meanings. In addition, attachments can carry viruses that can cause sudden damage to your computer. As a general rule, if you do not know the sender of the email, do not open attachments and delete the email. You are capable of blocking emails from the addresses you have selected. You can also make rules that block all emails that follow that rule, for example, block "Fraud" in any email subject.

E-mail is an information and communication technology. Today, e-mail uses tools to transfer a digital message from a sender to a receiver over the internet. There are many software platforms and applications available to send and receive. Popular email platforms include Gmail, Hotmail, Yahoo! Mail, Outlook, and many others. Yahoo, Gmail and Hotmail are not only top email providers but also offer 'real-time' messaging, or instant messaging which allows you to communicate in real-time through an application connected to the internet e.g. WhatsApp is a well-known instant messaging App.

Gmail

Gmail is a free email service developed by Google and is one of the most popular email service providers. It is used by most people, because of its security standards.

Google has given the facility of Gmail, giving electronic mail its trust and security. At present Google is world known for providing secure online facilities. Let's know what Gmail is and how we can use it for ourselves:

Gmail is a free email service developed by Google. Gmail makes email easy and secure. It embraces other Google services like Google Docs, Google Drive, and YouTube. You can receive, send, delete and store messages in Gmail just like any other email service. Gmail also suggests convenient ways to archive, search, and label. Let us learn how to get started with a new Gmail account.

If you have never had an email account before, Gmail is a good place to start. Moreover, it is reliable and free. For every account created you are given limited free storage of 15 GB that is spread across multiple services on Google, like Drive, Gmail and Photos. Your email is stored online, so you can access it from any device that can connect to the internet.

You may have to use G-mail at many places. This is known as one of your identities on the Internet. Through this, you can prove your identity in the online world. For this, a Gmail account is required. So, let's know where and how we can create our Gmail account. And we will also know what we need to do to create it:

How to Get a Gmail Account

To create a Gmail account, you must first go to Google and type 'www.gmail.com' in its search box. When the Gmail page opens, click on 'Create an account' to create a new Gmail account. After doing this, an online form will be displayed for you to open a new Gmail account. You have to submit it by entering your name, username and password. You will be asked for your phone number after submission. After confirming the phone number, your account will be opened by accepting certain terms and conditions. Enter your phone number and select 'Next'.

Google will then send you a text with a code that is required to be entered on the following page. Enter the requested information, and then proceed. Read Google's privacy information and select 'I agree' and then select 'Next'. After completing all the processes, your Gmail account will be opened, from where you can avail the facilities of Gmail. Once you get an account then you just have to sign-in to operate your account and then sign-out after using it. Gmail is an easy-to-use email App that saves your time and keeps your emails safe. To operate a Gmail account, you can also download the Gmail App from Play Store. After this, you have to open a Gmail account in your Smartphone with the help of your Id and password. All the features of Gmail will also be present in your mobile phone through the App. In App, you can get your mails instantly via push notifications, read and respond, and find any message quickly. Further, Gmail provides you:

- **An organized inbox:** Google Inbox keeps your mails safe in one place and keeps them in order. Here, you can see all the mails which have been received to you. Social and promotional messages are arranged into groups so you can read messages from friends and family as per your priority.

- **Sent mails:** All the mails you send are kept separate from the category of mails received. It is kept in a category called Sent Mails. Wherever you go, you can see as to whom you have sent messages, and can also confirm that they are delivered or not.

- **Less spam:** Many types of spam mails are also received on Gmail by many different companies, which can sometimes be harmful to the user. They are already filtered and placed in a separate category by Google Security. It gives you better convenience and keeps your today's mails separate from spam mails. Gmail blocks spam before it hits your inbox to keep your account safe and mess-free.

15GB of free storage: 15 GB of space is enough. With such a large space for email maintenance, you don't have to worry about its maintenance. Your mails will be safe here. You do not even need to delete mails to save space.

- **Multiple account support:** Yes, you can send a message to other addresses as well and receive the message from there itself. Use both Gmail and non-Gmail addresses (Hotmail/Outlook.com, Yahoo Mail, etc.).

Hotmail (Outlook)

Hotmail is a web-based service. That provides email service to its users. Hotmail is an email-facilitating website just like Gmail. With the help of this, you can send your message worldwide electronically.

Hotmail is one of the most popular free online email services provided by Microsoft. Hotmail is a webmail service and users can access it from any web browser anywhere in the world with the facility of internet connection, although it is necessary to know the username and password to use the Hotmail account.

The first free web-based email service, Hotmail was initially launched in 1996. Next year in 1997 Microsoft acquired Hotmail and then in 2012, Microsoft revamped Hotmail and renamed the service as Outlook.com.

Presently, the Outlook.com service provides virtually unlimited storage for free, connections to Facebook, Twitter, Skype, Google and LinkedIn, built-in search and spam filtering. You can also use Outlook to send and receive Outlook.com email. Outlook helps millions of users connect all their email accounts, calendars and files at one convenient place. Newly redesigned, Outlook allows you to do more from one powerful inbox.

It has a focused inbox that keeps the important messages on top. You can also switch between your email and calendar to schedule your next meeting, or share your availability with a few taps. If you wish, you can grab a document from your list of files and attach it to an email. With all this, you need only one click. Further, managing your busy days has now become easier.

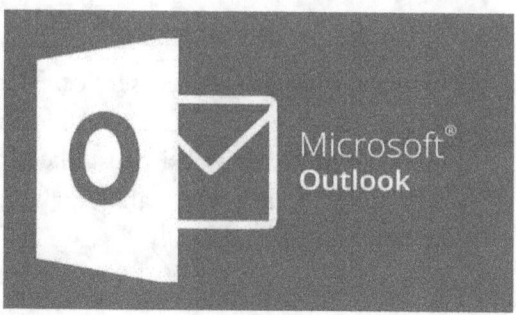

Like Gmail, Outlook also helps in receiving and sending the email. With the help of inbox facility, you can keep your received mails in one place. Outlook also has the facility of night mode, after which you can use it without any problem even in the dark of night. This makes the screen light much lighter, so that the user's eyes can be relaxed and work at night. You can search almost everything here; like any other user, files, documents, flight information, etc. can be searched here. There is also a calendar facility available where you can plan your events and mark them on the calendar by date after which the calendar will automatically send you notifications according to the date of the event.

If you want to use it on Android mobile, for this you can download an application named 'Microsoft Outlook' from Play Store. In this application, you will get all the Outlook's features on your mobile phone and you can use those features easily after creating an account. You just have to create an account after fulfilling the sign up form and submit it to the Outlook. After providing all details by yourself, your account will be created. Like the Gmail App, it is also very easy for users to use; it is an App similar to the Gmail App which has other types of features.

Yahoo Mail

Yahoo Mail provides email services like Gmail and Hotmail. It is famous all over the world for providing mail service to its users. It has over 281 million users worldwide. With this whopping number of users, it is the world's third largest email service provider. Like other email service provider companies, it also provides the facility to send and receive emails to their users. Their features are slightly different from other email service providers and also more interesting. Yahoo provides four different email plans: three for personal use (Basic, Plus, and Ad-Free) and another for businesses. As you get more out of the web; you get more out of life. Yahoo has made it easy for you to enjoy what is most interesting in your world.

Whether you need clutter-free mailboxes, additional customization, different views for deals, receipts and attachments or more storage, Yahoo has covered you in every situation.

It has a special structured inbox. You can sign in and start discovering all of the free organisational tools for your email. Its special thing is that it is very user friendly and easy-to-use. After a few uses, you will know very well as to how many features are available for your convenience and how you can use them.

You can also use it in your smart Android phone with the help of applications. To download Yahoo Mail, you have to install it by going to the Play Store and then taking advantage of this feature in your mobile. Mobile also has the same features that are on the website. Let's know in detail about some features in Yahoo Mail.

Features available in Yahoo Mail

Small in size: It's just 19 MB in size and very compact. It will take less time to get installed in your Smartphone.

Use any email address: You can login into another email account on this application. You can also add your Gmail, Outlook or AOL account and keep everything at one place. Custom settings, colors and desired notifications help to keep all your accounts separate.

Unsubscribe: Many times, we inadvertently subscribe to unsolicited websites or services. After which, we keep receiving mails from them. Due to the non-unsubscribing of such mails, they constantly send us notifications. Here, you get a feature to unsubscribe you where you can unsubscribe from unsolicited mail. You can conveniently unsubscribe the spam and junk mail which you don't want to let in your inbox. Yahoo Mail shows all the mailing lists you have subscribed to on one screen, and makes it easy to opt-out in one tap.

Customization: After you have been logged in on Yahoo! Mail, you can access the different customization options available. To do so, you may click on the "Settings" button that is located on the upper right part of the screen, right under the "Home" icon. Here you can access various customization options to change the platform according to your own liking and feel. By doing so, the messages from the theme's platform are displayed and are left in the inbox. You can deploy a menu showing various options to change the design and layout of the platform.

Travel view: Travel stress-free view keeps all of your flight information in one organized spot. Smart Updates, from gate changes to delays and cancellations, will instantly appear in the App, so once you check in you can check out.

Deals view: If you are a frequent shopper, you might like the Deals view, which transforms all of your promotional emails into an online shopping portal. It can list the top and favorite brands as per your habits and inclinations. Now, you can see the deals from your inbox in one quick view or enable location permissions to see a map of deals near you, and get notified in real-time as you walk into your favourite stores.

Groceries view: You can get the special and trending deals from your groceries, every time. Add your grocery store loyalty cards to save coupons. Further, see all the deals in your area and keep them on your shopping list to save even more.

People view: You can see emails from your favourite people and ignore the robot, the best way to avoid all unwanted computer-generated mails. Keep them separate by this amazing feature.

Receipts view: You can avoid crumpled receipts in your pocket and see them neatly organized in your inbox.

Notifications: You can choose from several categories of notifications, custom sound alerts and visual settings, for which you get the desired reminders.

Accessibility: You can access your daily habits; it provides access to all things, your stocks, your teams, your emails. Access is a part of everyday processes, so you can reach the world you usually love. It is optimized for use with VoiceOver and TalkBack screen readers. You can select a theme to change text and background colours for increased readability.

Hopefully, you have found some new and interesting ways to use email. Be sure to follow proper email etiquette when sending messages and watch out for Internet hoaxes.

Online Chatting

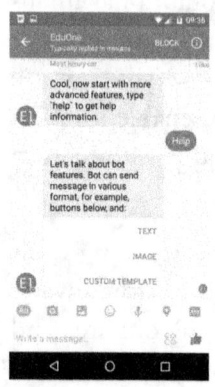 Chat refers to the process of communicating, interacting and/or exchanging messages over the Internet that offers a real-time transmission of text messages from sender to receiver. This involves two or more individuals who communicate through a chat-enabled service or software. When more persons are involved in chatting, messages are usually short so that other participants are able to respond quickly. Advantages of chatting include good time spent with friends and relatives instead of boredom. You also have a chance to make new friends and make your social network bigger. If you feel alone, or lonely and depressed, and you're looking to talk to someone about your problems or about your feelings, you may discuss random topics, your problems or other issues with other strangers on the internet.

Chapter 6

USEFUL APPS
FOR SENIOR CITIZENS

Simply put, an App (Application) is a type of software that allows you to perform specific tasks. Applications for desktop or laptop computers are usually called desktop applications, while those for Smartphones are called mobile applications. You will be excited to know that there are some Apps that can help senior citizens in many ways in your day-to-day life. I have found some of these useful Apps for seniors that will help you in every way to complete your routine life. These Apps for seniors cover all your needs like shopping, health, fitness, travel, education, and safety. With unique features these Smartphone elderly Apps are sure to benefit you in various tasks, I believe. Here, I will be explaining to you about some important Apps for the betterment of your life:

Some Important Apps for Senior Citizens:

1. WhatsApp
2. Skype/Zoom
3. Ola/Uber
4. Food Delivery Apps
5. Paytm
6. Doctor At Home
7. Drugs.com Medication Guide
8. Netmeds
9. Medicine time
10. Senior Safety Apps
11. Clap to find
12. Magnifying Glass + Flashlight
13. Dots–A Game About Connecting
14. Teamviewer App
15. Duolingo–Learning languages
16. Empowerji
17. Voice Assistant
18. Google Lens

1. WhatsApp

WhatsApp is a free App for Android Smartphones, iPhones, Windows Phones and Mac laptops and Windows PC. This application allows the user to send messages, pictures, voice recordings and even videos as well as make use of your mobile network to make voice and video calls over the internet for free. WhatsApp uses your mobile data connection, so it is worth noting if you are not connected to the internet. Without the internet, you were not able to operate or share anything. Just for your knowledge, a 10-minute video call uses around 5MB of mobile data.

WhatsApp can perform various tasks for you. I will discuss it later in the following pages. First, you should learn how to install WhatsApp on your mobile.

To download WhatsApp, you need a Smartphone with an active internet connection. Check the Internet and then open the Playstore App on your Smartphone. The Play Store is already pre-installed on Smartphones; you just have to click and it will open on your screen. Type keywords 'Whatsapp' and then click on search to find WhatsApp App. The App-icon will appear on the screen. Now, you have to tap on the WhatsApp official App and tap Install. Then tap 'Accept' after you review the information provided. Downloading will start processing and after downloading the process is complete, installation will start automatically. Now, 'Open' option will be there, just click and open the WhatsApp App.

Similarly, you may download and install any other Apps you wish to use from Play Store Apps. Process is the same, you just have to search and install on your Smartphone by following easy steps.

Once your Smartphone has WhatsApp, you are able to use it. Whatsapp requires only 10 digits of mobile number to activate your account on WhatsApp. To activate WhatsApp in your Smartphone after installing it, you just have to open WhatsApp App and click on the 'agree & continue'. This means you are agreeing to WhatsApp's Terms of Service. After click, enter

Read our Privacy Policy- Tap "Agree and Continue" to accept the Terms of Service

AGREE AND CONTINUE

your mobile number with country code (+91) and hit the 'enter' button. WhatsApp will use this number to verify your phone by sending OTP (One Time Password) to your provided number. Verify with received 6-digits OTP to confirm your number.

If you don't receive the 6-digits OTP msg., you should tap on the 'Call Me' button. This will place an automated phone call from WhatsApp to your number with your 6-digit verification code for confirmation. Note down your 6-digit verification code. Now, enter this verification code on WhatsApp. After successful account verification, your account will be activated. Now you can use it to chat, audio/video calls and you may share pictures, video, audio clips, files on it with any other WhatsApp users. Now, you have WhatsApp on your Smartphone. Let's take a view and see what it can do for you.

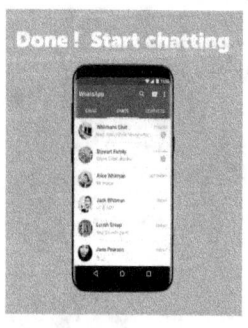

You can send a message: While SMS uses a cellular network to allow people to send short and urgent messages; WhatsApp needs a mobile network with mobile data or Wi-Fi to send and receive the messages. For sending a message, launch the WhatsApp App and click on the chat bubble on the top right hand corner. Then select the compose button which looks like a pen – and then select a contact from your list or type the name of the person you wish to talk to, and then select them. You will be presented with a chat screen. Tap on the white box and write your message. If you wish, you can also attach and share your own photos, videos, documents, location or even someone's contact details by clicking the clip like symbol to the right of the typing box. Click the rightmost icon, shaped like a paper plane, to send the message.

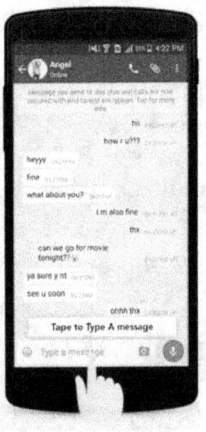

Interestingly, you can also send a Voice message. In order to do that, press and hold the microphone button, which is to the right of the text box, and speak your message. It will be sent as a voice note. You can also alternatively dictate your message. Tap on the white box to bring up your keyboard. Press the microphone button and dictate your message. The phone will automatically transcribe this into the message box.

Once you have sent your message, combination of coloured ticks in the bottom right-hand corner (A grey clock means you don't have an internet connection so the message cannot be sent at present, but it will be sent as soon as you do get a web connection. One grey tick indicates that the message has not been received yet, possibly as the recipient doesn't have an internet connection; two grey ticks means it has been received, but not read and two blue ticks means it has been read by the receiver).

You can turn this feature off so that people cannot see if their message has been read or not by heading to Settings. For this go to Settings, select Account, then select Privacy and then click on the slider next to Read Receipts to turn it off.

Delete a message: If you have sent a message by accident, don't worry. If it has not been read then you can delete the message.

Just press and hold, then select DELETE FOR EVERYONE and remove it from the chat. However, the recipient will see a message that says 'This message was deleted'.

Stop people seeing you are online: WhatsApp shows your contacts when you were last online (called a last seen). To see this, they just need to open the chat they have with you and at the top underneath your name will be the time you were last in WhatsApp. If you are using the App at that moment, they will see that you are online or the word 'typing' if you are writing a message. If you want to keep this a secret, then you can go to settings, then select Account, then Privacy, and then choose the option of Last Seen and select 'Nobody'.

Create a chat group: If you want to message a number of people at a single time so that you all can converse, create a group chat. To do this, press the Chat button at the bottom of the screen, followed by the compose button located in the top right-hand corner. Then select New Group at the top of the screen and select all the contacts you wish to add to the group. Select 'next' and then type a subject for the group along with an icon, which will be in place where the contact's photo appears. Then you can freely talk to all the people added to the group at once.

Make a call: WhatsApp also allows you to make video and voice calls. Press the Calls button (phone or camcorder icon) at the top of the screen. You can call someone in your contacts list.

Share a status: You can post images, videos and GIFs as a status that disappears after 24 hours, just like Facebook stories. Slide the screen to the left there and you will see two icons: a pen

& a camera. After clicking on the pen you will be able to write your own words and by clicking on the camera icon, you will be able to select a picture from your phone or take a new image. You can even annotate it.

Share your live location: In WhatsApp you can share your precise location with everyone. This feature will help seniors a lot. Open WhatsApp and press the Chat button. Tap the chat you're having with the person you want to share your location with, and then press the 'paperclip' icon and there you will find an option named 'Location'. Select that option and then click on 'Send your current location' to share your location. You can also click 'Share live location' for the amount of time you wish to share your location. Now, select the period and click icon on the right to share your live location for that period of time. Further, you can also click 'Stop sharing' at any time within that period.

Many times we find that the photo videos sent by another WhatsApp user in our phone are saved automatically. Actually, this happens because of the default setting of WhatsApp. To prevent photos and videos from being saved automatically, just go to Settings then 'Storage and data', there you will find 'Media auto-downloaded'. Now you can change it as per your wish.

Back-up your WhatsApp: Back-up is important. If you are moving to another Smartphone, or you need to factory reset yours, backing up WhatsApp will ensure that you don't lose any of your messages or call history from the App. Go to Settings, Chats, Chat Backup, and then select Back-up. Now you can choose the option to have WhatsApp data back-up daily, weekly or monthly automatically.

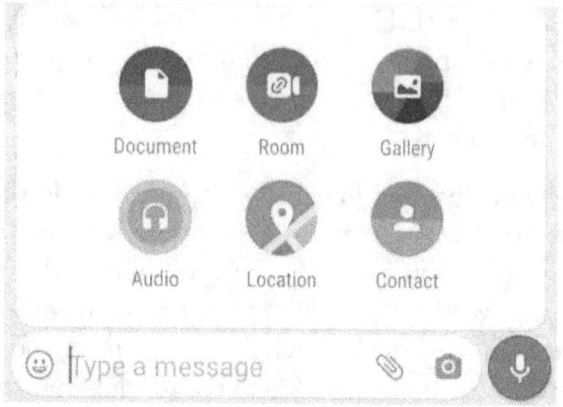

WhatsApp is a very easy and useful App for elderly people. They can enjoy this service and stay in touch with their loved ones at all times. Now you know a lot about WhatsApp. So, what are you waiting for? Pick up your phone and connect with your friends and families. Talk to them whenever you want and send your favorite photos, videos to them. This can help bridge the gap between young ones, providing better care, experience, and achieving more interaction. Now, you can easily stay in touch with your friends or family.

Here, you have learnt about the method of downloading WhatsApp from play store and the process to use it. Now you already know, in the same way, you can also download and install any other App on your mobile phone. You can also learn to download and install it with the help of any of your helpers. After this, you will know that there are so many other types of Apps available on play store, with the help of which you can make the tasks of your daily routine extremely easy. You can use those Apps better according to your convenience. Let's know about some other important Apps that should be on your mobile phones, and also discuss the subject of their utility one by one.

2. Skype/Zoom App (to hold video meetings)

Skype or Zoom App keeps the world talking. With Skype, you don't just hear the cheers; but watch them together with your friends and family on an HD video call. Watch everyone as they smile. You can also send photos and videos with your family and friends. And then you can save photos and videos shared by others to your device. You can also share your screen to make travel plans with friends or present designs to your team. You can use Skype and Zoom on your

phones, tablets, PCs and Macs. While on both of them you can do video chats and have the ability to record them, but they differ slightly on scale. Skype can only support up to 50 participants on a single video or voice conference. Zoom can accommodate up to 1,000 video participants and 49 on-screen videos. Use of the Zoom platform is free for virtual meetings, and video conferences of up to 100 participants, with a 40-minute time limit.

3. Ola, Uber, etc. (Cab-booking Apps)

Ola/Uber is an App that allows you to book a cab or auto-rickshaw to your location and take it wherever you need to go. They offer a variety of price ranges, sizes of vehicles, and even offer interstate travel. It also provides features like live location tracking, early drop, and online price update based on the distance travelled.

Online cab booking

Through technology we can make our daily tasks easier. Also, the work related to them can be done very easily. Travelling is

an integral part of our life. Many times, we have found that elderly people prefer to use private vehicles more. It is also comfortable and safe. Have you ever thought that if you do not have a personal vehicle or for any reason it is not available for you and you want to travel somewhere, then what to do? Most people will consider booking taxis, cabs, autos, etc. Booking the cab has also become very easy, nothing has been the same as in the past. Currently, technology is very useful. In today's technological era, every task is possible through mobile phones held in your hands. Just pick up the mobile and book a cab, taxi as per your need at home, without going anywhere. With only a few steps, you can easily book a cab and have the cab arrive at your location within a matter of minutes. Isn't it easy? The easier it sounds, the easier it is. All that you need is an application (OLA, Uber, etc.) to book a cab on your mobile and then enjoy the journey after completing all the booking process in just a few minutes.

Whether you are visiting friends and family, or just going to a nearby place of worship, sign up and enjoy complete freedom of mobility without depending on anyone. Feel free to use such kinds of Apps on the go. It is very easy and safe too.

Let's take a look at how these booking Apps are used;

To use Ola/Uber cab App, first of all, we have to download and install this application on our mobile phone through the

Play Store. After the installation completes, it will ask you to enter your number and email ID to register you as a user and confirmation. After the account is created, you can use any mode of payment, such as debit card, net banking, etc. Alternatively, if you want, you can also pay through cash at the end of the journey. For this, you have to select 'Cash after ride' option.

To book a cab in these applications, you have to show your pick-up location and then enter the drop location, where you want to visit. After that different options of cabs will pop up on the screen. From those categories, select the cab category as per price which suits you and book the cab. At the end of the booking process, you will get complete details of cab, driver and navigation showing real time location of cab in your mobile. After booking the cab, you will also be provided with the cab driver's number so that you can contact them, if you want. After the cab reaches the place you have chosen, you will receive a call from the cab driver for information. It will show a 4 digit OTP. Once inside the cab, you have to provide the OTP to the driver to start your journey. It is safe because people share their trip details with someone you trust so that they can track your trip on a real time basis. Enjoy your ride, for any questions/help, contact customer helpline number.

How to book a cab ride in advance for a later date

Traveling has become very easy due to the online cab booking process through Ola/Uber. Those days are gone, when people,  especially elders without a private vehicle, were supposed to rely on state transport services or rental cars. As we already know back in time, booking private cabs was not as easy as it is today, thanks to growing Smartphone consumption that has opened up some new ways to deal with these kinds of things. Booking cab ride is usually a simple task, but it is slightly trickier to pre-book rides for a later date or time. So, let us take a look at how to book a cab ride in advance. Advance booking has many benefits. Let us say if you are trying to book a cab, it is likely that no cabs would be available at that particular time. Hence, booking a cab in advance will help you in the crunch time as the cab will show up at your pick-up location at specified time, and get you to your desired place on time.

To book a cab in advance you just have to keep some points in mind. Always make sure to have an updated Ola/ Uber App on your Smartphone. In case you want to update, go to the Play Store and search for Ola/Uber cabs App. You can update the App over there. Once you have the updated Ola/Uber cabs App installed on your phone, go to the App and login into your Ola/ Uber account. After you have successfully set up your account, open the App. You will then be able to see your current location on Google maps with a Pin on the screen. Then you just need to move the pin to the location of your desired pick up. It is the location where a cab driver will come to pick you up. You can also type in your pickup and drop locations. There will be two options to choose from: Ride later and Ride now, at the bottom of the screen. Since you want to book a cab ride in advance, you need to tap the 'Ride later' option.

Once you have hit the Ride later option, you will be asked to choose your preferred date and time when you want to be picked up from your location. It is worth mentioning that Ola/ Uber allows users to pre-book the ride only 1 hour 15 minutes before starting a journey. So, choose a time accordingly. You will then be asked to confirm your ride details that include your pickup/drop locations, total fare (depending on the type of cab you have opted for) and pick-up time. You can also choose your mode of payment from options like Ola/Uber money, debit/ credit card, cash, etc. Confirm your ride, and then you will get a confirmation that your ride has been scheduled. Details about the driver who is going to pick you up, will appear on the App 15 minutes before the scheduled pick up. In case you want to cancel or view your ride details, you are allowed to do so. Cancellation process is also easy to just click ride details and tap cancel. Once you have successfully cancelled your ride, you will be notified that your booking has been cancelled. By doing this process you can avoid the hassles at the time of booking a cab, and be sure to book your cab beforehand.

Book Cab without Internet Connection

Many times, we are in a place where it is very difficult to get an internet connection, due to which internet facility is not available. Has it ever happened that you open the mobile and the internet is not working, or the network data is exhausted? Yes, it happens often, but what can we do if we want to book a cab during that time? Don't worry; there is another process to book a cab. It is quite easy and you can book your cab without the internet. There are some easy ways to get a cab booked. The process was very simple.

Open Ola/Uber App and opening the Ola/Uber App without the internet connection will show up two options: Try Again or Book via SMS. Select the second option it will redirect you to your default messaging application to send an SMS to a particular number. Just send a message to that number and wait for some time. Within no time, you will receive an SMS showing the details of all the cabs around you. Choose one of them and reply to it with the cab number. As you wait for confirmation, you will get an SMS with all the details of the cab heading your way. Thereafter, the driver will be given your details and location as well. After this process, your cab will be booked without the internet.

4. Food Delivery Apps - Swiggy, Zomato, FoodPanda, etc.

You can order food online from restaurants and get it delivered at home!

With the increasing use of Smartphones, now you can have almost everything in just a few taps. And this applies to food as well. You can order all kinds of food online; from any restaurant you like and have it delivered to your location within a short time, depending on your location. If you feel hungry and want to order tasty, affordable and exciting food at home, Swiggy can prove to be a great App for you. This makes your

main doorstep folded delivery. You will have to download it from the Play Store to have Swiggy party through you. Then, from there you can get your favorite food and drink ingredients to your house in a very short time. The main reason for the popularity of Swiggy is its strong delivery network that ensures quick delivery of your orders. You can also live track the person delivering the food to your home.

There are various other big companies and startups that are trying their best to make food delivery service better.

There have been a plethora of food delivery services in the market recently. While some were limited to certain cities, some are now available in different cities offering quality food delivery service to its customers. The biggest Apps are competing with each other by giving discounts and different kinds of additional services. They are usually location based and show you which food outlets are open nearby and who can deliver to your exact location. Like previously mentioned, some also allow you to live track delivery person's precise location, so you know exactly how long you will have to wait to receive your order.

The best apps providing these services are Swiggy, Zomato, FoodPanda, Uber Eats, Just Eat, Domino's Pizza, Freshmenu, Faaso's, etc. Some cities like Bangalore and Mumbai have plenty of services that are only delivering in small areas or limited in a specific city. If you

have a better experience with those, you can keep on ordering. If you prefer a well-established food delivery service, you can choose for the bigger names.

Here you get many types of facilities

Food per your mood: Are you in the mood for a hot coffee, a nice biryani, Cheesy pizzas and sumptuous burgers or some salad & juices? You will find all your favorite food & beverages on these Apps. They can deliver over 30 cuisines at your home ranging from North Indian, Afghani, Chinese, South Indian, and even many foreign cuisines such as Korean, Thai, Vietnamese, Mediterranean and American. Healthy or junk, street food or luxury food, local or global, breakfast or late night cravings, you will find every food option. You can enjoy a variety of foods here as per your mood.

Long Distance Orders: Most of these food companies are quite serious about their work. They also take food (very) seriously. They deliver from restaurants not just that are near you, but also from those faraway places and those even farther from you. And hence, oftentimes, to get to your favorite restaurants, they don't mind travelling those extra miles too. After you order food, your food will reach you properly and fresh.

Lightning Fast Delivery: Many of them are committed to delivering your food, piping hot and fresh. Their Delivery Experts are spread across every corner of your city, and they meet their targets on time. They even deliver food late at night, at the same lightning speed.

Live Order Tracking: No more calling the restaurant to check if your order is prepared or picked. Further, you will be able to live track your delivery right from the restaurant to your doorstep. In one place, you can get all the information about your ordered food.

Freebies, Cash-backs, Offers, and Discounts: You will always have an opportunity to avail many offers and discounts with restaurants, banks, credit/debit cards, UPI and wallets, making your food more affordable.

Pay instantly, on delivery, or later: If you want, you can pay online for your order and at the same time, you can pay at the time of delivery using cash after receiving the ordered food.

You may pay instantly using VISA/MasterCard Credit or Debit Cards, Net Banking, Paytm.

5. Paytm Wallet

Think about a situation, you bought something from a shop and while making payment, you found that there is not enough money in your purse to take those goods or you have forgotten to bring the money. What would you do in such a situation? In such a situation, if you have an ATM card, then you will consider going to an ATM because your money deposited in your bank can be withdrawn from the ATM card. But when you reach the ATM, you find that there is a very long queue to get the money from the ATM machine, or the machine is out of order. And think once, what will you do if you do not even have an ATM card?

As we know, technology is making our work and all the tasks related to daily routine easier. Presently we buy many goods throughout the day, and pay them with the money kept in our purse. No work/purchase is possible without a transaction of money. Whether we buy or sell things, money transactions are important. Technology has made our payment process easier like all other things. Yes, it has been made possible. Today, with the help of technology, we can make any kind of payment directly from our mobile phone without putting money in our purse. Paytm is India's most popular e-wallet application.

With this help, you can avoid the long line of ATMs; it also gets rid of the process of withdrawing money from banks. And most importantly, there is no fear of losing money because it is digitally safe in your mobile. Just a few clicks and money will be released from your account for payment as per your order.

By the way, many types of mobile applications exist for the payment of money. Withdraw your money from the bank and keep it safe in the mobile application, and pay it easily and securely if needed. You can use these applications for all types of payments, either big or small.

Let us now know one of these most reliable and secure applications. What is Paytm App? You would first like to know how we can use it, how it works and also take a look at some other important points related to it.

Paytm is India's largest mobile payments and E-commerce platform. This is a very useful application for all of us. This App is used for money transactions. With Paytm, you can transfer money to any person or vendor at zero cost. It provides a lot of convenience to the elderly by making the payment method easier. You can use it to pay for many services like taxis, autos, grocery stores, petrol pumps, restaurants, shopping malls, coffee shops, parking, pharmacies, hospitals and local shops. You can also use it to pay bills online like utility, electricity, telephone, mobile, water payments, book tickets for movie/theatre or purchase travel tickets for bus, train or flights and the list is endless. Today the number of daily active users on Paytm is over 39 million and their number is constantly increasing, it is safe and easy too.

As we know and are well aware of this problem, the heavy rush of people to withdraw money at ATM and banks can be tiring & time consuming at the same time. Not having cash in hand can block many of your purchases, thereby, creating a hassle in day-to-day life. To overcome with these problems, now say goodbye to in-hand cash worries by making the use of Paytm Wallet. If you are not carrying money in your pocket wallet, then you can use Paytm Wallet and shop as much as you want. The transaction done through this platform is safe and there are minimal chances of failed transactions.

First, you need to set up an account with Paytm. The account creation process is simple. It just requires your mobile number and email ID.

How to open a new Paytm account?

You can download the Paytm App on your Smartphone by Google Play Store or go to its website www.paytm.com. For Android users, you need to go to the Play Store and search for Paytm App & tap 'Install' to download the App on your Android device. For Apple users, you must go to the App Store and tap the magnifying glass on the bottom right of the screen. Search for Paytm App and tap 'Get' to proceed with the Paytm App installation on your iOS device.

Simply, open the App and easily sign up by entering your mobile number, email id and desired password. You can change the password and other details. Paytm will send OTP or Confirmation code to your mobile number. Enter that code to confirm your mobile number and afterwards, you will be taken to your Paytm profile page. There you will have to enter details like your name, email id and other information for completing your profile. Then you can verify your email by going into your email inbox.

How to make payment through Paytm?

Paytm allows you to add money to your Wallet through options like debit card, credit card and Net banking or ATM card in the most convenient manner. Without KYC, there is a limit of Rs 10,000 per month on transactions using the wallet. You can increase the spending limit by getting the KYC process done. For doing that, go to KYC option, and follow the steps given. It will give you a list of stores nearby where you can go to complete the KYC process or you can arrange doorstep KYC in which someone from Paytm will come at your house to complete the process.

How to pay someone using Paytm?

- Open the Paytm App & select 'Pay or Send' option

- Scan the recipient's QR code or enter their mobile number in the 'Pay' option of your Paytm App.

- Enter the amount you want to transfer, add comments if any and tap on 'Pay'. Your money will be instantly transferred from your Paytm Wallet to the recipient's Wallet.

You will receive a confirmation on your registered mobile number once the transaction is complete.

How to use Paytm without the internet?

You can use Paytm for payment even if the internet is not available; you just have to follow some simple rules to adopt the process.

To do this, Paytm has launched a toll free phone number–0120-4456-456

To use this method you have to call from your registered mobile number to 0120-4456-456. You will hear a voice message letting you know that you will get a call back to set the PIN.

After the PIN is set, you can easily make all your payments offline by calling this number, entering the phone number of the recipient, then typing the amount, and finally confirming your PIN.

Now, you got to know how to pay using Paytm. So, what are you waiting for? Start using Paytm Wallet and make payments from anywhere while travelling or from any location at any time. In addition to that, you can avail several coupons when making those payments, which give you discounts and benefits on other purchases.

Paying through Paytm is quite safe and easy. You can make any type of payment through the Paytm App like mobile recharge, water, gas & electricity Bill Payment, DTH recharge, book IRCTC Train, bus & flight tickets, LIC insurance premium payment, money transfer, metro card recharge, pay stores with QR code scanner too and many more. For any kind of assistance and help you may connect with 24x7 Customer Care (0120-4456-456) for all your queries and concerns.

6. Doctor-At-Home

 Those who prefer natural home-made remedies for some common diseases, this App will help them a lot. You can download the 'Doctor at Home' App on your Smartphone by Google Playstore. It is the best Android App for quick, safe, and effective treatment of more than 100 diseases naturally. Using this App you can potentially solve your problems at home, and even get information on all diseases and symptoms. You can also learn to use natural herbs as medicine alternatives, home treatment and natural cure for stomach, hair, skin, respiratory, circulatory, head, jaw and teeth, bone/joint, eye, and many other diseases. You may search diseases by categories. It can also be used in Offline mode. You can then share treatment with your friends and family.

This App has some great features, with the help of which you will be able to use it best and correctly. It is very easy to use. This App will be liked by people who want to cure minor diseases with home remedies. So, let us have a look at some of the features given in this App.

Features

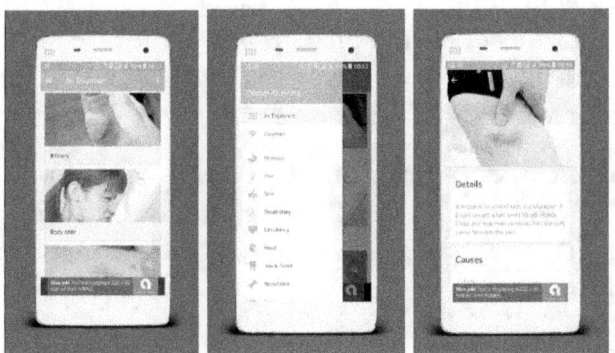

Home treatment for more than 100 ailments: You will get home treatment for over 100 ailments in this App, also methods of home remedies for physical problems and other important information about those diseases. The entire method of treatment is natural.

Quick search treatment/diseases: The names of all diseases are written in a sequential manner and are quite easy to find. To find any disease and its treatment, you can find the disease through its name or with the help of the photo given.

Diseases by categories: Here you can also search for any disease on the basis of the category for information about its treatment. All the diseases present in this App are divided into different categories. Such as - stomach, hair, skin, head, teeth, eyes, bones, etc. With the help of these categories, you can get the information directly to the right disease and its treatment easily.

Add to favorite: If you want, you can put any treatment/ disease in your favorite category, after doing this, you can search for all types of treatment related to that disease in your favourite category without going to search it again. Suppose you feel a toothache. The instructions mentioned in this App helps to relieve you from ache. In such a situation, if you want, you can put that treatment in your preferred/ favourite category, so that in the future, if you have pain in your teeth again, you can find that treatment without delay.

Suggest diseases for natural treatment: In the past, home remedies were used to cure almost all diseases. This art is very ancient; it has become extinct in the modern era. But even today, there are many such people among us who are aware of the home remedies of many diseases with methods to make them. Many elderly people still believe in such treatment methods.

If you have the knowledge of some similar home remedies, and know well how to make them and you want to share it with the world, through this application you can make it reach the world. This is quite easy to do and this knowledge given by you, will be added to this App for everyone's use.

You can send home remedies and its method to the owners of this App by email. To do this, after opening this application, you will see three vertical dots on the top most right corner. After clicking on those dots, you will have to click on 'Suggest Treatment'. After doing this, this App will take you directly to the Gmail App, where you can write your methods and send it to the concerned person.

Share treatment with your friends and family: You are well aware of the benefits of home-made remedies. Many of you may have also tried some home remedies. You will get many such kinds of home-made treatment instructions in this App. Many times our loved ones also suffer from similar minor illnesses. In such a situation, you can also share them (confirmed by you) remedies with this App to help them. This sharing process is quite easy. All that you have to do is to click on the share icon (top right corner on App screen) and choose the medium through which you want to reach your loved ones, and then send it to them. This is the treatment method that will reach them.

Offline: The special feature of this application is that you can also use it without the help of the internet. Use this application and take advantage of the remedies given in it even without the internet.

7. Drugs.com Medication Guide

Daily drug users often have difficulty in how to control the timing of medication, and may also be aware of the side effects caused by taking different types of medicines at a time. Especially the elderly have to face such problems every day. To reduce some of these problems, an App called 'Drug. com Medication Guide' is available on Play  Store. There are many types of features available in it. These are specially made for those who take medicines daily. Using this App is the easiest method to lookup drug information, their dosage, and the best time to take them, check interactions with other drugs and set up your own personal medication records. This App has many useful functions for senior citizens to use as explained below:

My Med List: It is very difficult to take different types of medicines at the right time every day; most of us forget to take medicines. This feature is made for such people so that you can take all medicines without forgetting at the right time. You can leave the rest of the work by simply typing the name and duration of taking the medicine in this App. You can add your medications to organize relevant medical information in a simple, easy-to-analyze format. Dig into in-depth consumer data, news alerts, plus food allergy and medical condition interactions with each other. It is an invaluable tool for medication management and adherence.

Here, profiles of different people can also be made based on age/gender. It works offline too.

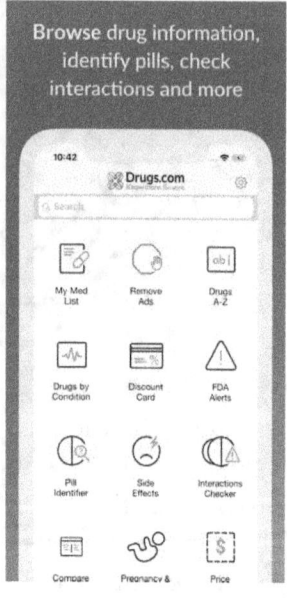

Complete Drugs A to Z listings: Information about different types of medicines is available here. You can find medicines by name and according to that name, you will get all the information available. The resources have been provided to help narrow your search to specific, targeted drug information. Information is available for both consumers and healthcare professionals on over 24,000 prescriptions and over the counter medicines. Fast search, accurate suggestion engine and the most comprehensive database of drug information are available online.

Pill Identifier: People taking daily medicines often keep their medicines in a particular box so that right medicine can be taken on time without forgetting. Often we have seen that the medicine pills remain open in the same box, or get separated from their packet. Usually, we forget what the pill is, and should it be consumed? At this time, medicine has to be thrown. But with the help of the feature pill identifier given in this App, you can find outwhich company is that medicine. All you have to do is to enter the imprint of the medicine in the App. If you want, you can search it according to the shape and colour of the pill. On searching, you will see results, in which the photo will be present. You can get information about your medicine by clicking on the photo that matches your pill. This database is updated daily by the App.

Pregnancy & Breastfeeding: Some medicines are safe to take during pregnancy while others may have adverse effects on the unborn baby. It also has features according to pregnancy and breastfeeding. If you want, you can get some information here too. However, this situation is a very sensitive matter. According to this, medicines and precautions should be taken according to the doctor's prescription. Always consult your doctor or health specialist for medical advice regarding the use of the drug while pregnant or breastfeeding.

Interactions Checker: Anytime you take more than one medication, or even mix it with certain foods, beverages, or over-the-counter medicines, then you are at risk of a drug interaction. Drug interactions are usually not serious, but it is extremely helpful to know about cases when they can be serious and potentially life threatening. Let's take a view on how it will help you to check on the basis of different kinds of interactions:

Drug-drug interactions: These are the most common type of drug interaction. The more medications you take, the greater the chance for your drug to interact with another medicine. Drug-drug interactions can decrease how well your medications work, may increase minor or serious unexpected side effects, or even increase the blood level and possible toxicity of a certain drug. For example, if you take pain medication, like Vicodin, and a sedating antihistamine, such as Benadryl, at the same time you will have an additive amount of drowsiness as both medications cause this side effect.

Drug-food/beverage interactions: You have probably seen the stickers on your prescription bottle to "avoid grapefruit juice" at one time or another. This may seem odd, but certain medications can interact with foods or beverages. For example, grapefruit juice can lower the levels of enzymes in your liver responsible for breaking down medications. Blood levels of an interacting drug may rise, leading to toxicity. This interaction can occur with the commonly used statins to lower cholesterol, like atorvastatin, lovastatin, or simvastatin. The result can be muscle pain, or even severe muscle injury known as rhabdomyolysis.

Drug-disease interactions: Drug interactions occur not only with other drugs or foods but also with other disease. Your existing medical condition can affect the way a drug works For example, over-the-counter oral decongestants like pseudoephedrine (Sudafed) or phenylephrine (Sudafed PE) may increase blood pressure and can be risky if youearlierhave high blood pressure.

This App provides a list of interactions that may occur when different drugs are taken at the same time. It also checks food interactions automatically.

The Symptom Checker: Symptom Checker is to help you understand your medical symptoms and make informed decisions about your health and wellness. Lookup specialized databases for side effects and dosage information. Confused about the spelling of a drug? You may use the phonetic search.

Q & A: Any question might be coming in your mind. Enter your questions directly using its Q & A feature. Many questions and answers related to your question will be in front of you. Ask a specific question about your medication. You may search on thousands of questions and answers.

Health Professionals: It has quick access to all the tools that you know and trust.

8. Netmeds App

We all have to take medicines to take care of
our health; these medicines should be taken
only after the doctor's prescription letter.
To buy the medicine recommended by the
doctor, we directly go to the pharmacist and buy the medicine.
When the medicines are exhausted after a few days, we have to
go back to the pharmacist to take the medicines again. Now you
do not need to go out of the house to get medicine. It helps you
by delivering medicines to you without leaving your home.

When you are short of essential medicines, it can negatively
impact your health whenever your medicines run out; you can
directly get those medicines sitting at home at a good price
through the Netmeds App. Netmeds is one of the best choices
for seniors to keep track of their medicine schedule and order
them online, if needed. In this simple App, you just have to
add your prescriptions to place an order. All the medicines sold
here are prescribed and approved by doctors. With the help of
Netmeds, you can get your medicines easily from anywhere, at
any time. You have to just open the App, upload your required
medications, and your order will be delivered anywhere in India.
By downloading it, you can order your medicines online in a
very convenient way. Using this you can also purchase and send
medicines anywhere in the country with just a few clicks. In
addition to ordering medicines online, there are many more
features in this App. You may use the Netmeds healthcare App
to Order/Refill Your Medicines, Consult a Doctor Online, Store
Your Medical Records, Track Your Order, Rate Items, Check
Reward Points, Refer Your Friends.

Netmeds offers a range of medicines and over-the-counter
items, like vitamins, supplements, essentials, herbal products,

pain relievers, mother care products, beauty care products, and much more.

Netmeds App key feature: Netmeds App ensures a quick, easy, and user-friendly ordering process while saving your time and money.

Buy medicines online: Doorstep Delivery is available. It is the only online pharmacy to deliver to any location in India. Discount is also attractive on medicines. Money-Saving Medicine Deals is active on this App 24/7.

Consult best doctors online: Need FREE Follow-up Consultation? Have an urgent medical question? Here you are advised by specialist doctors. If you are feeling unwell and want to contact a doctor online then you can contact them here. This App can help you. With Netmeds App, you can instantly Call/Chat with top specialist doctors online across India from anywhere, at any time. Opinions are provided to you by trusted doctors from all over the country.

Freeaccess to health information: Get easy access to the reliable medicine information at your fingertips. Explore a wealth of trustworthy health information that's designed to help you make better decisions about your health.

Timely medicine refill reminders: Most of the time, we get information about the out of stock medicines only after seeing the empty packets of medicines. This happens to almost all of us, especially with the elderly, due to which many times our doses of one or two times are missed. If the medicine is being used to relieve pain, then in such a situation, the patient may have to bear the pain, which may become unbearable at times.

But Netmeds will remind you about all the medicines that you are using before they are over. You can order your medicines before they are over and use them regularly without forgetting and prevent any untoward incident.

When you are about to run out of your medicines, Netmeds will send you an alert to restock your medicines. Just one click and your stock will be refilled.

Find all about your order: You can conveniently track your order status in real-time, straight from the phone in your hand! Further, you can view your order history or see reward points and notifications in your Account. Netmeds provides customers with a superior online shopping experience, which includes ease of navigation and absolute transactional security. Just instantly upload your required medicines & leave the rest to Netmeds dedicated pharmacists–they will reach out to you promptly.

Netmeds provides customers with a superior online shopping experience, which includes ease of navigation and absolute transactional security.

Just instantly upload your required medicines & leave the rest to Netmeds dedicated pharmacists–they will reach out to you promptly. Shop with Ease & Save Your Time!

9. Medicine Times-Pill Reminder & Medication Tracker App

Most of us often forget to take our medicines at the right time. Mostly, the elderly often face discomfort due to forgetting the time of taking medicines and they missed it one or two times. This happens to almost all senior citizens. If this happens to you too, there is nothing to 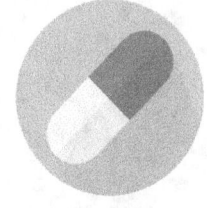 worry about, My Therapy App is present in your service. My Therapy is a pill reminder and medication tracker. With the help of My Therapy, you can set an alarm by prescribing the time and dosage of medicines. It will notify you via notification when it is time.

With this App, you will not forget your medicines again. Download this App and let it remind you. You can change the time of reminder for each specific day of the week. It even keeps an inventory of all meds to let you know when you are almost out so that you can contact your doctor or just swing by the store (depending on what you're taking!). A soft bell will ring and a pop up notification too will appear on your set timings. It is very simple to use and functional for elderly people.

To set a reminder you have two options, you may click a picture and upload it or choose the icon for the reminder. If you didn't upload any pics, the icon will be applied automatically for your convenience. Thereafter you will have to set a date, duration to take medicine and at what interval. After uploading all this information, you just have to enter the name of the patient to set a reminder.

10. Senior Safety App

Senior Safety App is meant to be installed on phones carried by Senior Citizens. The caregivers of senior citizens are sent safety alerts through monitoring options via control panels connected to the internet. This App is popular with caregivers, concerned children of seniors and elderly care homes too.

In this App, you can monitor phone location & activity remotely over a web browser. With a GPS tracker, this App helps you keep track of your loved ones, with alerts for emergency help requests, spam Apps, phone damage, phone inactivity for a long time, Apps installs or uninstalls on the device, entry/exit from specific areas (buildings, streets, cities or neighborhoods), SIM card change and low battery alerts.

This App is to be installed on the senior's Smartphone. Caregivers use their email on the program and they can review alerts and reports via online console at https://account. seniorsafetyapp.com

The App allows calling to reach one of the emergency contacts, among the options; to ensure help is provided on time, even if some of the contacts may not answer their phone. The purpose of this App was to help the elderly lead an independent life while being connected with their loved ones at the click of a button.

This App is very simple to use and easy to understand. It is a powerful tool for elderly people's help. This App contains some valuable and advanced features, which are designed to provide better facilities to the elderly, such as:

SOS & Alarm: This ensures quick request help when needed. SOS is an option available on the App in the task list. Selecting this option sends out a text alert to all the contacts in the App, along with the current location of the device. There is a single click option to call all emergency contacts one by one until the phone is answered. It includes a powerful alarm function for attracting attention during emergencies.

24/7 Senior GPS tracker: You can monitor the senior's phone remotely from your dashboard to track current location and location history of up to 90 days. You can keep an eye on your elderly loved ones and ensure that they travel safe, get their exercise and stay out of dangerous situations.

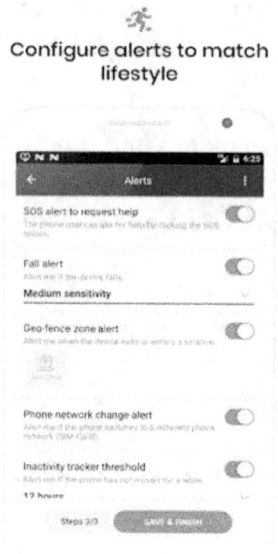

Configure alerts to match lifestyle

Fall Alert: If the phone user was to either have a fall or a sudden jerk while walking, climbing stairs or driving, the cell phone will send out a message to the caregiver. You can adjust settings to send an alert to a predetermined contact. The message that is sent through both text and email, gives the time and location of the fall with the GPS tool embedded in the App. The settings can be adjusted according to the lifestyle of its user.

Geo-fence Zone Alert: You will receive alerts when the device leaves or enters a pre-configured geo-fence area, such as a neighborhood, a town or metropolitan area. While going to a particular place, the information about the entry & exit with the location is sent via email to the caregiver. It promotes safety and security.

Inactivity Tracker: If your loved one, who is a senior citizen, lives all by themselves, this is an extremely important feature that alerts the family or friends if someone has been immobile for an extended period of time. The time and length for inactivity can be adjusted based on a person's sleeping schedule and a particular lifestyle.

Low Battery Alert: Cell phone is often the only contact with the outside world for many seniors; hence, keeping it charged is of utmost importance. You can configure when you want to get alerts based on battery availability.

Malicious App Report & Alerts: You can review a list of Apps that are in use on the phone with the time spent on each, receive an alert whenever a brand new App has been installed or removed from the mobile, which poses a threat to the device or the user. Malicious Apps have become common-place with some that are specifically targeted to seniors.

Emergency Medical Information: Often the details like doctor's name, phone, medications, allergies, and other relevant medical information remain unavailable during emergencies.

Senior Safety App guarantees that relevant help is provided to people who need it in case of an emergency. The Senior Safety App is popular with assisted living facilities, home healthcare companies and healthcare workers working with elderly people across the world.

11. Clap to find (phone)

Most of elderly must have felt that we keep our things and forget it somewhere, especially mobile. Sometimes you forget to put it in a bag, sometimes it is hidden under a pillow on the bed, sometimes it is laying between books and files. When needed, they keep looking for it and waste a lot of time. But the mobile  phone is sometimes in such a place that it is not easy to find it. What to do in such a time? The 'Clap to Find' App is at your services. Finding mobile has been made very easy through this application. You can install this application on your phone from Google Play Store App and it will help you find your device quickly.

After installing the App, you have to tap quickly with your hand three times. Clapping will initiate a loud alarm even when the phone is in silent mode. Along with the sound, the phone will also turn on the flashlight and begin to vibrate to help you find the phone with ease. When the tap sounds, the mobile will automatically indicate its location to you. These signals can be by various means such as loud sound, continuous vibration and flashlight; this will help you find the phone in the dark also. Now you don't need to waste much time to find your phone. You can find your phone in seconds without getting worried.

12. Magnifier - Magnifying glass with light

Have you ever been in a sticky situation where you are in a restaurant and cannot read the small print on the restaurant menu or have trouble reading instructions written on medicines? There are many magnifying Apps available in the Play Store that can help you magnify what you read even outside of your phone.

Magnifier allows you to turn your mobile phone into a magnifying glass. You don't need to carry a magnifier anymore.

Just download the Magnifier App in your Smartphone, and you will be able to read even the tiniest print clearly. Further, you will see everything big and clear. Best of all, you will stop blaming yourself for your imperfect eyesight. In addition to getting the best magnifier, you will also get the brightest LED torch flashlight. You have to simply turn on the magnifier and watch as it auto focuses the text, while providing you the ability to zoom in/ out further. The image or text is enlarged via digital zoom, and it also provides additional lighting (turns your camera flash into a torch) to make the text even more readable. Moreover, you can click photos and save the magnified photos on your phone. Thereafter, you can browse saved photos and can also share or delete them.

13. Dots - A Game about Connecting

Dots is one of the best game Apps for seniors, a beautifully addictive puzzle game about connecting the dots. All the illustrations and skill of quick thinking help improve hand to eye coordination  and are lots of fun. The game is simple: connect same-coloured dots vertically and horizontally to win points. Make a square to win even more! Everyone can play alone, or with other players of this game online.

Dots include three main modes that suit everyone's taste. Race against the clock in Timed Mode (connect as many same-coloured dots as you can in 60 seconds), think strategically in Moves Mode (kick back & take your own time making the right moves), or sit back and relax in Endless Mode (relax and play; the no-limits, gravity shuffling mode of dots).

14. Teamviewer App

There is another App called Teamviewer App, which, if installed on your phone allows you to control other devices, and vice versa also. It means that your kids or grandkids or some other close family member can, if required to help you out by using your phone if you are stuck. Of course, there is a safety aspect linked here as you are giving control of your device, and hence there is a code attached. Unless you share the code with the concerned people as per your need, they cannot do so. So, many people living apart are keeping this option in their phone to use in case of emergencies.

15. Duolingo - Learning languages

Duolingo is a free language-learning program. It is a fun game-like App for learning languages. Its appealing interface helps anyone learn a new language of your choice in an exciting way, and fulfill your bucket list. This App offers about 32 languages including Hindi, English, Spanish and Chinese making it an ideal senior citizen App. Duolingo is the best application that makes language learning available to everybody. Seniors will find it very exciting.

16. Empowerji

Empowerji is the best way for senior citizens to get comfortable with electronic gadgets and technology. It is specifically designed for senior citizens of India. This App helps them to learn how to use tech. You can learn how to use Apps and Sites in simple videos. There is no need to be dependent on your family or friends to teach you. Empowerji is rooted in the ideology that technology makes self-reliant, so you should embrace it. Its vast knowledge sharing makes you more self-reliant by turning you into a tech-savvy.

The Empowerji App helps older adults learn how to use Apps, Sites & more so that they can live happily self-reliant lives. This App is available in 4 languages—English, Hindi, Marathi and Gujarati. Most importantly, everyone can learn at his own pace. You can learn from simple step by step videos, enjoy curated features and showcase your writing and photography work with the community.

The Empowerji Assistant (EA) service is a combination of a Personal Assistant + Caretaker Service + Yellow Pages. Seniors can contact the assistant to get support on tasks or to get service or to learn about anything. They can call for anything and will be guided to the next step. So, in case they need to book a cab–the EA can book it for them. If they need to order medicines or book a Doctor's appointment – the EA can handle that, if they need to decide where to buy a gift or what to purchase–the EA will take care of that as well.

17. Voice Assistant

Depending on which phone you are using, you can use voice assistants like Siri, Alexa, Cortana, or Google Assistant to make its use easier. In Android phones, all you have to do is to just hold the phone close and mention "Hey Google." And the voice assistant will be activated. On Apple phones, you have first to enable it through the settings. Once installed/ configured, all that you need to do is to talk to your phone to make it do things and need not navigate it. For example, you can ask for information, or ask it to make calls or send messages, or even guide you back home from anywhere. You could also get reminders set for taking your regular medicines or making a doctor's appointment, etc. Almost any command can be given, and you can get a response from the voice assistant.

18. Google lens

 Google Lens is a highly advanced application, with features that you can use to point your phone camera at something, such as clothing, shoe or accessory, and then let Google Assistant explain to you what it is you are pointing at. Along with an answer, you will also be guided exactly where you can get a similar product nearby, like at a shoe store or clothing store. Google Lens helps you recognize restaurants, clubs, cafes, and bars, too, presenting you with a pop-up window showing reviews, address details and opening times. It's the ability to recognize everyday objects that are impressive. It will recognize a hand and suggest the thumbs up emoji, which is a bit of fun, but point it at a drink, and it will try and figure out what it is. Further, Google Lens offers the following interesting features:

Translate: You can point your phone at text and, with Google Translate plugging in, live translate text in front of your very eyes.

Smart Text Selection: You can point your phone's camera at text, then highlight that text within Google Lens, and copy it to use on your phone. So, for instance, imagine pointing your phone at a Wi-Fi password and be able to copy/paste it into a Wi-Fi login screen.

Smart Text Search: When you point to a text, or select a text in the image you took, Google lens can define that word for you and even translate it into your specified language, if something is written in a popular language that you don't understand.

Shopping: If you like something you saw in the mall or a store, Google Lens can help you identify the product and tell you options about where you can get that for yourself. This works for household decor and more, too, via relevant reviews and shopping options.

Search around you: If you point your camera at your surroundings, it can identify objects in your area. It means identifying the kinds of plants, breeds of pet cats, models of an electronic device, and highlighting text/reviews of DVDs from our entertainment stand.

You can also download many more Apps of your choice by visiting Play Store.

Hopefully, these essential Apps for senior citizens will enhance your life and enable you to live with more independence and excel your life post retirement. Embrace technology instead of fearing or avoiding it as we live in a digital era where technology should be accessible for seniors, ageing parents and grandparents.

Uninstall Apps from the Play Store

As you now know Apps are necessary for better facilities in Smartphones. Installation is an easy process. All Apps work according to our needs. But what happens when their need is finished, or you don't need to use too much of an App? In such circumstances, you can consider uninstalling that particular App. This is also very easy to do after which the App will be permanently deleted from your mobile phone and then you will not be able to use that App. Let us understand the process to uninstall Apps.

Tap and hold the icon of the app you want to delete and drag to the top of the screen where you see 'Uninstall'. Or you can go to settings, then to Apps. Thereafter select the App, you want to delete. Tap 'Uninstall'.

You can also uninstall the Apps by going to Play Store. On the search box there, search by name for any App you want to remove from your mobile. In search results, you will be able to see that existing App on your screen. After that, you have to click on that App. App will open with their details. Now, you will see two options there. 'Update' and 'Uninstall'. To uninstall, all you have to do is to click on the option to 'Uninstall' and then click 'OK' for confirmation. After doing this, the uninstallation process will start on your mobile, after that desired App & its related files will be removed.

CHAPTER 7

ONLINE
& MOBILE BANKING

Online banking, also known as internet banking or web banking, offers customers almost every service traditionally available through a local branch including loans & deposits, transfers, and bill payments. Mobile banking refers to the use of a Smartphone or other cellular devices to perform online banking tasks while away from your home computer. The online banking or the Internet banking provides almost all personal banking features, such as viewing account balances, obtaining statements, making fixed deposits, checking recent

transactions, transferring money between accounts and making payments to third parties. While Internet Banking allows you to conduct online transactions through your PC or laptop and an internet connection, mobile banking can be done with or without the internet.

As mentioned above, money can be transacted through an online banking system. But most of the elders believe that online banking is a complex process, and money is not safe during this time. And above all, they got this fear that some tech-savvy smarty may steal financial information if they join the population of online banking customers. At the same time, there is also the fear that their slight negligence may cause them to lose their money. Such fears are further encouraged by the fraud cases coming occasionally on the news-channels/social media. This fear is also justified as it can be risky to use any technique without caution, but due to this fear, it is not appropriate to avoid online banking.

Through online banking, the elderly can do the normal working of their bank without going to the bank and without wasting time. This is the easiest process to monitor your money in the bank accounts. Now take a little comfort in this, online banking is more advanced and secure than ever. Banking facilities are so accurate and easy to handle that now a growing number of seniors are able to manage their money from the house. In online banking, you are provided with many types of facilities. You get flexibility and convenience. Online banking allows you to view your account balances, pay your bills, location of nearest ATMs and transfer funds to other accounts, with or without an internet facility.

Kind of equipment we need for online banking

Ideally, you need a computer, laptop, tablet or Smartphone with updated security software. You may also visit your bank's official website and register yourself according to their terms and conditions. You can use your Smartphone too for banking operations.

You will be able to do everything online that you do at a local bank. Almost all the basic and sometimes advanced features are available on the official website. You will be able to manage all your banking, credit and financial accounts in one place. No doubt it is a fast and easy way to look up your current account balances, but you can also view your past account history.

Time taken to register account online

That depends on your bank terms and conditions. In many cases, it is as simple as filling out a short form online. You will need some information at your fingertips, including your account number and some other identifying information, so the bank can confirm it's really you signing up for your account. In many cases, it is a process that takes only a few minutes to register you for online banking.

Cost in fees to handle online banking

Charges in online banking are even less than direct dealing. Most of the banks do not charge monthly maintenance fees. Since you don't have direct dealing with bank branches, you save money on operating costs compared with traditional banking.

Most banks also prefer you to use the online and mobile banking tools they provide because it allows them to meet your needs without having to keep a branch open 24/7. Most importantly, the online services are generally free of charge.

Banking with a Smartphone!

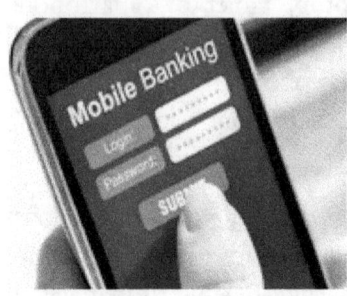

With a Smartphone, you can easily operate your account wherever you are, rather than at your couch or kitchen table at home. Further, many banks offer free mobile phone Apps you can download that allow you to check your balances, transfer money and pay bills, etc.

Further, banks are held to a high standard when it comes to protecting your money and personal identity information. All banks have to follow RBI guidelines to create multiple layers of protective security in their online banking system, and regulators who assess these institutions further ensure that your bank is meeting their stringent security requirements. Your bank also has a vested interest in ensuring that the online banking systems, whether PC- or mobile-based, are fully secured.

Delivering financial services through electronic channels is a cost-effective also and competitive way for your bank to do business. Each and every effort has to be made on securing those systems, and making them safe.

Nevertheless, you as an individual also play an important role to ensure that all your financial information is fairly safe. While more and more banks are deploying security technologies that try to assess if anything is wrong with your device before allowing you to log in to online banking, it is equally important to ensure that the computer or mobile device (Smartphone or tablet) that you use for online internet banking, is protected.

You may have a question in mind: can anyone who has access to your phone use your banking App? The answer is no. Only you can log in to your banking App by using a six or eight-digit PIN that you are asked to set at the start. Just like your ATM PIN, you need to keep this PIN confidential. On the App's home screen, you will be asked to enter this PIN, and only then can you access the bank's App and your account details.

Most importantly, online banking websites are protected using end-to-end strong encryption technology, which ensures that even if you are using an unsecured wireless access point, the information and data being transferred between your laptop and the bank is completely encrypted, and therefore not viewable by any malicious person in between. But it is important to understand that there are potential risks associated with using unknown and unsecured wireless (Wi-Fi) access points. Using and maintaining firewall and antivirus software on your computer is important when using public Wi-Fi hotspots, and at the same time, you should avoid using any Wi-Fi hotspot you are not familiar with, for banking.

You may ask which is more secure: banking by computer or by mobile phone. The answer is that both of these channels are safe and secure if you take the appropriate basic precautions on your computer or mobile phone. In the world of computers, the operating system software that makes them work has been improved and made more secure over time. As long as you follow the general rules of online computer safety, they provide a safe online banking environment. Your mobile devices (smartphones or tablets) have the advantage of running relatively new operating system software, which has been developed with strong security in mind. Mobile banking Apps are generally more secure than other Apps.

YONO SBI App (Online banking with SBI)

YONO (You Only Need One) is an integrated digital banking platform developed by the biggest public sector bank, State Bank of India (SBI), which enables the bank's customers to avail various financial and other services like online shopping, taxi booking or medical bill payments, etc. YONO has been introduced as a smartphone App for both Android and iOS.

YONO SBI is Quite Safe

Just like any other App/Web based platform introduced by the State Bank of India, YONO is completely safe. Not only YONO, various Apps by State Bank of India such as SBI anywhere, SBI quick, etc., and also Apps of other Banks are launched only after ensuring foolproof security.

Through this application, almost all the facilities of the bank can be available to you on your mobile. It is quite safe and reliable as well as has been made very easy to use by account holders. You can take advantage of this application without any fear, and can always find yourself linked to your bank and their facilities. Let us take a wide look at the facilities provided to the account holders in this application:

Apps overlook is simple and user friendly. You just have to login before using this App. For security reasons, you have to generate 6 digits' PIN Id and then the App will allow you to link with your bank account. Process is very easy and will be done in a few minutes. As mentioned earlier, this App has almost all the features of the bank, like:

Account: You can get information related to your accounts with State Bank of India. Information about the amount available in your existing accounts, bank mini statements, etc. will be easily available to you.

Deposit: The process of opening a Recurring Deposit (RD) account, getting a Fixed Deposit (FD) takes a lot of time as well as customers have to travel to banks for this. But, at this place, you can get your account fixed, and also open an RD account in no time. Money can be deposited directly from your saving or current account in a fixed deposit or RD account opened by you. This process is quite easy. Moreover, you can have overdraft facility online against your deposits.

Insurance: Insurance facilities are provided by the bank. All the procedures related to insurance have been greatly simplified by this application. In this App, you can also add your old policy. By doing so, the payment for the old policy can be made directly from the money deposited in your own SBI account. This is the simplest way to ease the payment process of insurance. Here, you can also apply for new insurance. The YONO application provides its users with the facility to apply for two types of insurances. The first is life insurance and the second is general insurance. In General Insurance Motor Insurance, Personal Accident Insurance, Health Insurance, Travel Insurance & long term home insurance is done. All that you have to do is to apply here and the remaining information will be available from SBI bank.

Loans: An attempt has also been made to make the process of obtaining a loan easy here. The account holder can apply for a loan from SBI bank. Loans are provided by SBI Bank for various purposes. Through this application, you can fill the application for home loan, car loan, education loan and express credit loan. The application form given for applying for a loan is quite simple. You can fill it in a few minutes and can send it directly to SBI bank through this App. Here you also get an EMI calculator with which you can get information about the EMI for the loan. Along with this, details of the loan have also been made available and after applying, all the process to get loan approval has also been explained.

Credit card/debit card details: Here you can track your SBI credit card details. Also, apply for a new credit card if you don't have one. You may link your account with SBI credit card for further payments.

Investments: If you want to invest by SBI Bank, through this you can prepare your portfolio in different types of mutual funds and get all the information related to them. You can invest directly with the money in your account. This is the best way to get details about New Fund Offer (NFO). You can also open a new Demat and trading account, and can also link your old Demat account for more facilities.

Shop & order: SBI YONO also provides you shopping platforms. New and best offers to purchase various brand products are available here. Attractive discounts and deals are on orders. You may also book your train ticket and pay through this App very easily.

Services request provides you to manage PIN, block ATM/debit card, activate SMS alert, stop Cheque, profile setting, password setting, request status, pension details with form 16 (part B) and much more facilities.

The SBI YONO App is providing so many facilities to you through a single App; with SBI trust and security features it becomes very comfortable to use. It is very helpful for senior citizens, making payments though it is very easy and they can monitor their account too without visiting a bank on a regular basis. But, if you still have any kind of problem then you can stay connected with the Customer Service Officer for 24 hours to all your problems. They will try their best to solve in time. For any help, you can connect official and toll-free number 1800-11-1101 and for emergency/fraud number 1800-11-1109.

Till now, we have considered almost every important point related to online banking. Along with this information, you also need to know that some precautions should be taken while using online banking. By taking these precautions, you can protect yourself from digital thieves. So, let us know what you should do and what not to do to secure your online banking.

Safety tips for online banking

Do's

- Ensure that you have shared your mobile number with the bank and select the Mobile banking option in the form. If you are an existing account holder and have not yet registered your mobile number with the  bank, you can do so by visiting any branch of your bank or by visiting any ATM with the help of your debit card.

- Keep changing the PIN from time-to-time.

- In case your mobile phone gets stolen or lost, contact your bank's customer care immediately and report the same.

- Keep your mobile phone locked with a password, so that no one else is able to use it.

- Lock your mobile phone screen when not in use.

- Download the Mobile Banking App only from authorized stores like Google Play store.

- In case you have changed your mobile number, inform your bank immediately.

- Check your account statements regularly to keep an eye on any unauthorized transactions.

Don't

- Do not share any secret information about your PIN or bank account details with anyone.

- Do not transfer money without verifying the credentials of the receiver.

- Do not keep any sensitive information like card details or PIN in your mobile phone.

- Switch off your phone's Bluetooth when not in use.

- The bank will never call to ask details about your card, PIN etc. Do not fall prey to such calls.

Automated Teller Machine (ATM) provides us the facility to deposit cash-money into your account and withdraw cash money from your account at any time. This facility offered by the bank is also very reliable and secure. You can easily withdraw money from your account through your card and through confidential PIN code. This machine is very easy to use; it can also be used by the elderly without any hassle. It is so safe that banks are now providing the facility to customers through this to deposit money in their account or any other person's account. The ATM is very easy to use and using it once or twice will give you the confidence to use it regularly as required.

There have been some cases of fraud at automated teller machines (ATMs). To make sure that you don't become a victim of any ATM frauds, you must follow some precautions:

1. You should not take any help from strangers while using the ATM.

2. If you notice somebody right behind you or at your side when you are transacting, please request them to move away. While entering your PIN on the ATM,  cover the movement of your fingers on the PIN pad with the other hand, purse, book, mobile or any other thing that you may have with you. This will ensure that even if people try to see the numbers you are pressing on the PIN pad or there are hidden cameras near the ATM,

capturing your hand movement and PIN; they will not be successful. Nowadays almost all banks' ATMs have a 'PIN shield' which is like a flap on both sides of the PIN pad. This is mainly to protect your PIN entry from the hidden cameras.

3. If an ATM site is in a remote corner of the street and looks desolate, avoid using it especially during night time. Find a brightly lit and well-kept ATM. ATMs in India are typically located in 800-1000 sq. feet outlets nearby banks, depending on the branding of the bank to which they belong, while others are located in lobbies of corporate buildings, airports, malls, etc.

4. Please don't enter ATM outlets if you find people inside. If they are using the ATM, let them complete their transaction. But if they are just loitering inside, ask them to move out. Further, if you suspect something fishy, leave the site immediately.

5. If you have to urgently withdraw cash, before starting the transaction, check your surroundings and the ATM for any hidden camera. Look at the card reader. If you see something looking abnormal, tug at the card reader to check for any 'skimmer' attached to the card reader (Skimmer is a device to read your card data, skimming is a trick where scamsters steal your debit/credit card data and clone it. They then use it for siphoning money off your account.) To clone your card, scamsters set a camera or duplicate keypad in order to record your PIN number. You should also check the slot from which cash comes out of the ATM and if you see anything suspicious then don't use the ATM.

6. Never give your card or PIN to anyone, even to your

own child, spouse or sibling. There have been many instances where a cardholder's relatives have defrauded the cardholder using card and PIN. It is also possible that your child, spouse or sibling is not aware of the precautions to be taken, and due to any other person's negligence, you may land you into trouble at any future time.

7. Many fraudsters loiter around ATMs, trying to act as good helpful people. They talk sweetly to you, watch you enter your PIN and memorize it. They intentionally pull out your card from the card reader and switch the same with a look-alike card which they give to you. You may not notice that you have got the wrong card. Once  you leave the site, these fraudsters use the card obtained from you and the PIN noted by them to empty out your account.

8. Some fraudsters have even more maneuvers on it. They install a small camera on the inside part of the flap. So, if you see ATMs that have flaps on either side of the pin pad, please put your hand under the flap and check for any hidden camera. Please stand as close to the ATM as possible. This will ensure your body covers the activities you do on the ATM and nobody from behind is able to see your account balance, your PIN or cash amount you are withdrawing.

9. You should promptly count the cash you receive, put it in your wallet or bag, press the cancel button and wait till the ATM screen shows the 'Welcome' screen before you move away. This ensures your transaction is fully completed and no one can access your account through your card and PIN.

While withdrawing cash from the ATM is a simple process, you can make it safer if you keep in mind the above mentioned precautions in mind.

By taking such small precautions, you can somehow avoid any forgery. This common information can protect you from cheaters and fraudsters. You must scream aloud when you are the victim of fraud or feel it. Give the ATM Guard a voice to help you. You should always be careful and stay safe.

Chapter 8

DIGITAL WELLNESS & CYBER SECURITY

Due to the lack of cyber security awareness and training, most senior citizens may not have an idea that fraudsters and criminals are trying to get their personal or financial information. However, as seniors become more digitally savvy, there is a need to explain how to be safe online.

Today, with young adults moving out of the country for work or business, senior citizens are jumping onto the digital bandwagon to stay connected to their loved ones. And, with the rise in digital payments, scamsters and fraudsters who have been eyeing this space have come up with their own version of clones to target gullible users. Older people get isolated and lonely, and these are the two prime ingredients capitalized on by cyber-criminals targeting this demographic.

However, cyber theft and online fraud is no longer a new thing. Primarily this was done through blackmailing, ransom and spam calls to people in their age group. With the increased adoption of technology, online frauds such as internet crime, cyber threats, and hacking have also increased considerably. According to a recent report from Help Age (a senior citizens organisation), a staggering 60 percent of respondents believe that the use of social media has resulted in increased economic loss. Hence, it has become crucial to stay safe from such fraudulent practices, especially with one's identity and financial credentials that are used so vigorously online.

Almost all of your life's earnings may go into a hacker's account within minutes just because of a lack of awareness. How can they do this? What mistakes are we making that we fall prey to them? Even after finding the answers to all these questions, you are not able to get them and even if you get answers, it is very difficult, if not impossible to bring back the money withdrawn from your account. We are cautioned about online fraud everywhere. On TV, in the news, by the bank, by the government and other related departments, the public is told about the ways to avoid online fraud. Till date, we have not understood clearly how the hackers get access to our mobile/laptop and obtain our confidential information. It appears strange, how can anyone enter our mobile/laptop and control our device!

Let us understand, what is hacking? How do they hack? And what does it mean? In the following paragraphs, we will try to find answers to such questions and know how all these can be avoided.

Hacking is the process of gaining unauthorized access into a computer system done through cracking of passwords and codes which gives access to the system. It has often been seen that hackers try their best to hack into any mobile by contacting them in any way. The medium of contact can be anything; by SMS, by call or WhatsApp message, by email, by any online form, etc. Most of the calls or SMS are received for providing any type of service, relieving you of any hassle or getting the KYC done at the bank or insurance company.

Currently, a trend is going on . Hackers call/message you (target) and say that you have not done KYC in this App threatening that your App will be closed. You receive a fake SMS. It is made so accurate that it is difficult to recognize at a glance that this SMS is from a fraud. These hackers send such messages to many people at once; in that message, it is written that we are the officers of the respective customer care and if you have to do KYC to continue the service provided, then you can call the number given in SMS. As soon as you call the number available in this message, on the call, someone talks to you in a very simple and decent manner and says that he will get your

KYC done promptly, but for this, first of all, you will have to download/install a particular App suggested by him. They urge you to download their App.

It is worth noting that the target is often asked to download a particular App. They force you to download the App because it is an easy way to enter your mobile or laptop. He asks you to download a simple App from  the Play Store, such as: Anydesk remote control, Teamviewer quick support. This App is used to control mobile/laptop. Their names are so similar that most people get cheated that it is really getting downloaded to support by customer care executives so that no one could doubt. You download the suggested App. Now this App is installed on your mobile/device and at the same time, it is also installed in the hacker's device.

Hackers from the other side inform you that they will guide you through this App and facilitate you. To connect your screen to their own screen, they will ask you to tell the code that came on your device screen and then to request it. When you do this, your screen will be connected to the hacker's screen. This is the easiest way for hackers to connect your screen to their screen. After that, they can control your device completely through their device, view and control your screen, view your messages, save files from your phone to their own device and also view your photos/videos. Even the OTP message on mobile can be easily seen by hackers through your screen. Today, mobiles/laptops have become an integral part of life. It has personal details, payment transaction details and all bank details. In this way, all the confidential information related to your life and accounts is available and just think once, what will happen if some hackers get all this information. After that, you will be able to know only when and how much loss you are suffering.

Further, by creating a small form on Google Form App, a form is prepared by putting the logo of any reputed institution/organisation. Hackers put this form on the Internet to find their target. As soon as someone clicks on that form link, they say that a transaction of say 2 rupees is mandatory for customer support. In that form, you are asked to fill information related to your bank such as: - Name, UPI PIN, Account Number, ATM Card Number, Expiry Date, etc. As soon as you fill your information in the form, pay the requisite amount online and submit it, all the details provided by you reach the hackers in a very systematic way. As soon as you do this, you provide that hackers a pipeline directly from your bank account. After that, they can withdraw the money from your account immediately as desired. Also please remember, no bank officer, executive of Wallet App can ask for any information from you on phone call. It is completely illegal.

Nowadays, hackers have provided their numbers in the names of reputed departments and institutions. All these numbers were processed in a wrong way to reach the first number on the Google search list. For example, suppose you are looking for the number of any hospital (AIIMS hospital) and you searched on Google by typing the name of the hospital ("AIIMS hospital appointment number"). On searching, in the first place, you will be shown the name and contact number of that hospital. When searching from mobile, we can directly click on that number and call. As soon as you contact the number, that call reaches to the hacker by that edited fraud number. On call, you say that you have to book an appointment at that hospital. And then the hacker tells you that

to book an appointment, he is sending you a form, by paying 2 rupees, you can book your appointment. Subsequently, after filling the form received by you, you pay the asked amount. In such a situation, the payment you made without thinking once, and made it available all bank-related information; the hacker withdraws all the money from your account. Therefore, to avoid these kinds of troubles, do not search Google to find any specific number. Always find the number on the official website and call only the number available there.

Presently the Government of India has made available a national website and a portal www.cybercrime.gov.in, where you can immediately report about such kind of fraud. If you want, you can also go directly to the police station in your area and give information about such suspicious activity in the shape of a complaint. If the police action is started promptly and effectively, then withdrawal of money from your account may be stopped, or may also be returned before reaching the hackers.

As soon as you realize that you have been cheated online, you can make some important decisions:

1. Call the bank's customer care and request them to immediately block the card and bank account.

2. Change your UPI PIN immediately, so that it is difficult to conduct further transactions.

3. Delete/uninstall that App.

4. Put the phone on airplane mode.

5. Inform at www.cybercrime.gov.in.

6. Go to the police station and give a detailed complaint.

7. Follow Twitter/Cyber Dost is an initiative of the Ministry of Home Affairs for spreading awareness about cybercrimes.

After losing money digitally, it becomes very difficult to get it back and the chances of recovery also become bleak to a great extent. That is why it is necessary to follow cyber security very seriously, so that you do not lose your lifetime earnings by getting caught in the fraud of any kind of online scam or enticing opportunities.

Below are some simple cyber-security best practices for my senior friends to follow and stay protected from cybercrime:

1. There is no person or company waiting to give their fortune to you through a lucky draw. Hence, never click on suspicious-looking or too-good-to-be-true offers.

2. It might seem like the easy thing to do – but using the same password on every service and App is a bad idea. You should use unique, strong passwords on every site and App that you use.

3. This one might sound like a no-brainer, but don't share your passwords with your son/daughter, relatives or friends either. It is simply because if the account of the person with whom you have shared your password gets hacked, then you can be followed too.

4. If your friend wants to use the same App such as Facebook or a banking App, log out from your App, and they should get their own account that's under their control and login through that.

5. Forgotten by many, but make sure to always password-protect your mobile phone or any other device

you use especially while traveling. And lock it when you are not using it. You should use two-factor authentication on your accounts to keep hackers out.

6. Never share your personal information including your full name, your birth-date, and also your location.

7. Always log out! Make sure that you don't leave any account open when you go away from your computer, mobile phone or any other device.

 Many of us begin our mornings with WhatsApp. And then as the day progresses, it is time to check Facebook, now and then to keep track of what everyone else is doing. All this till yesterday was no more threatening than the number of hours we lost in keeping pace with social media. All that changed recently when it was revealed that companies like Facebook have been using our data, selling it to a third party and based on your behavior, showing us news and ads that influence our decision-making.

Not only is there ethical consideration to our social media habits, but it also makes us wonder what else might be happening with the information that we share online. Every 'like' and every 'share' might be sending signals to potential influencers about us and our behavior.

However, there is no need to just delete our account and wash our hands of social media. If we develop a safe social media habit, we can still enjoy its benefits while safeguarding our data online. In today's globalized world, children are moving out of town and even countries, leaving their parents back in the Homeland.

Social media platforms such as Facebook, WhatsApp, FaceTime, Skype and various other Apps have made it easier to stay in touch. Not just that but with the help of technology, ordering groceries and medicines, paying bills, booking appointments and other transactions can be done easily, not to forget that some Apps are even great for passing time.

It is rightly said that not everything is Rosy in the world of Technology. Some primary concerns with technology can be:

1. Breach of privacy

2. Lack of online security

3. Chances of fraud and hacking

4. Mishandling or faults with online money transfer and payments

5. Fraudulent website and viruses

However, this issue should not stop you from using Technology effectively. Instead, educate yourself about safe online habits and surf the internet without a single concern.

How can you make online shopping safer?

With each passing day, online scammers across the globe are becoming bolder and more creative. Quite recently, Delhi

 CM Arvind Kejriwal's daughter was duped by an online scammer of Rs 34,000 while trying to sell a second-hand sofa on the popular sale-purchase online platform OLX. Once the person agrees to deal virtually, the scammers send a test bar code for the target to scan. On the first go, the victim receives a small amount of money in their account upon scanning the bar code. Once the victim is convinced that there is nothing fishy, they send the second bar code which is designed to debit and not credit the money. As soon as the victim scans the second bar code, the scammer deducts money from the victim's account. In some cases reported online, the scammers even emptied the bank accounts of unknowing people.

Once you are on the Internet, you are pretty much in contact with the rest of the world. This can prove to be both good and bad. However, you can safeguard yourself from the bad to a great extent by:

1. Not giving out your personal information and details. This code includes your address, phone numbers on social media. Some delivery-based applications may however need you to provide such information.

2. Not using very obvious passwords such as your children, Grandchildren's name, date of birth, etc. Also, avoid using the same password across different websites and handles.

3. Checking your privacy settings. On social media, you can choose to make your account public or private. For example, you can make your account private on Instagram by just visiting your profile and clicking on the top right bar. It will take you to settings where you can choose

to stay private by activating the private profile option. On Facebook, anybody can visit your profile. You can, however, choose who views your status, pictures, etc. on the setting page located on the top right corner.

4. Not talking to strangers on social media; it will be better to block the stranger as soon as you receive a friend request/follow request from them. Visit the profile of the person and click on the block option.

5. Giving out your bank/card details to any trusted website. If you are shopping online, try to choose the cash on delivery option. This way, you do not have to provide financial details at all. Transfer money online through a wallet with a secure payment gateway.

2020 Twitter bitcoin scam

On July 15, 2020, a number of high-profile Twitter accounts, each with millions of followers, were compromised in a cyber attack to promote a bitcoin scam. At some point, roughly half that sum in bitcoin was withdrawn from the account. The scammer asked individuals to send bitcoin currency to a specific cryptocurrency wallet, the tweets involved in the scam hack claimed that the sender, in charity, would repay any user double the value of any bitcoin they sent to given wallets, often as part of a COVID-19 relief effort. More than 12 bitcoins were sent to one of the addresses involved, the equivalent of more than US$110,000. Minutes after the tweets were posted; more than 320 transactions had already taken place on one of the wallet addresses. Investigators from all over the world stepped in immediately with the goal to identify types of exchanges and freezed the funds on different accounts.

How to identify suspicious activities?

1. No website will ever ask you for your PIN number. Online payments use the OTP method for transacting. If you are asked to provide your PIN number, it is a significant sign that it is a trap.

2. If there is a complicated jargon used to get any real information, it is often fake and intent to mislead the user.

3. Mail offering you too-good-to-believe schemes is always a fraud. They usually claim to give millions of rupees for no apparent reason or provide you with a lump-sum loan on properties. Such messages should not be believed and immediately deleted.

4. Messages or statuses asking for monetary help are often a trap. Hackers try to get the sympathy of people by spreading messages that "say so and so be admitted in hospital and need money for treatment please transfer to...."

What to do in case of the occurrence of a fraud?

Prevention is always better than cure. However, if you happen to end up being a victim online in any way, you can do the following:

1. If the scam involves money, immediately call your bank

and inform them of the (fraudulent) activity. In some cases, they may be able to reverse the transaction and get some money back. RBI has  come up with new guidelines favouring customers that if customers fall victim to frauds, their respective banks need to compensate some of their loss immediately, if they are informed within a specific period of time. Further investigation will then be carried out.

2. If your privacy is breached on social media platforms, report the person, you suspect is responsible for it. You can do this by clicking on the report option in their profile and mentioning your cause of concerns with them in the provided dialogue box. They will be blocked immediately.

3. If you are a victim of online abuse, do not put up with it. Troll comments, or comments that are hard to get a response from you, are widespread these days. Report these people to the social media platform. If things get really complicated, be sure to take a screenshot of the entire conversation, and if needed, report to the police & cyber crime cell.

Simply put, with just a few simple steps, you can ensure that you are not cheated online and that your privacy is a safeguard. For more information, you can read each social media channel's help-guide or even ask someone you trust for help. Wish you all the best.

Notes:

Notes:

Notes: